TestSMART ™

for Reading Skills and Comprehension—Grade 4

Help for
Basic Reading Skills
State Competency Tests
Achievement Tests

by

Lori Mammen

These popular teacher resources and activity books are available from
ECS Learning Systems, Inc. for Grades PreK–6.

The Bright Blue Thinking Books	Gr. 1–3	3 Titles
Building Language Power	Gr. 4–9	3 Titles
Foundations for Writing	Gr. 2–8	2 Titles
Get Writing!!™	Gr. K–5	6 Titles
Home Study Collection™	Gr. 1–6	18 Titles
The Little Red Writing Books	Gr. 1–6	3 Titles
Math Whiz Kids™	Gr. 3–5	4 Titles
Novel Extenders™	Gr. 1–6	7 Titles
Once Upon a Time™ for Emerging Readers	Gr. K–2	10 Titles
Once Upon a Time™ (Books + Tapes)	Gr. K–2	10 Titles
The Picture Book Companion	Gr. K–3	3 Titles
Springboards for Reading	Gr. 3–6	2 Titles
Structures for Reading, Writing, Thinking	Gr. 4–9	4 Titles
Test Preparation Guides	Gr. 2–12	41 Titles
Writing Warm-Ups™	Gr. K–6	2 Titles

To order, contact your local school supply store, or write:

ECS Learning Systems, Inc.
P.O. Box 791439
San Antonio, Texas 78279-1439

Editor: Jennifer L. Sullivan
Cover: Kirstin Simpson
Book Design: Educational Media Services

ISBN 1–57022–199–5

Printed in the United States of America.

Contents

> ## Welcome to *TestSMART*™!!
>
> It's just the tool you need
> to help students review important reading skills and
> prepare for standardized reading tests!

Introduction

During the past several years, an increasing number of American students have faced some form of state-mandated competency testing in reading. While several states use established achievement tests, such as the Iowa Test of Basic Skills (ITBS), to assess students' reading ability, other states' reading assessments focus on the skills and knowledge emphasized in their particular reading curriculum. Texas, for example, has administered the state-developed Texas Assessment of Academic Skills (TAAS) since 1990. The New York State Testing Program began in 1999 and tests both fourth- and eighth-grade students in reading.

Whatever the testing route, one point is very clear: the trend toward more and more competency testing is widespread and intense. By the spring of 1999, 48 states had adopted some type of reading assessment for students at various grade levels. In some states, these tests are "high-stakes" events that determine whether a student is promoted to the next grade level in school.

The emphasis on competency tests has grown directly from the national push for higher educational standards and accountability. Under increasing pressure from political leaders, business people, and the general public, policy-makers have turned to testing as a primary way to measure and improve student performance. Although experienced educators know that such test results can reveal only a small part of a much broader educational picture, state-mandated competency tests have gained a strong foothold. Teachers must find effective ways to help their students prepare for these tests—and this is where *TestSMART*™ plays an important role.

What's inside this book?

Designed to help students review and practice important reading and test-taking skills, *TestSMART*™ includes reproducible practice exercises in the following areas—

- vocabulary
- comprehension
- study skills

In addition, each *TestSMART*™ book includes—

- a master skills list based on reading standards of several states
- a comprehensive vocabulary list
- complete answer keys for multiple-choice questions
- scoring guidelines and rubrics for open-ended questions

©ECS Learning Systems, Inc.

- a reproducible answer sheet

The content of each section of *TestSMART™* is outlined below.

Vocabulary: This section of *TestSMART™* includes 12 practice exercises with questions that focus on—

- demonstrating knowledge of synonyms (Practices 1–3)
- demonstrating knowledge of antonyms (Practices 4–6)
- using context clues to determine word meaning (Practices 7–9)
- recognizing the correct meaning of a word with multiple meanings (Practices 10–12)

(Note: Vocabulary skills addressed in this section are also addressed in the reading comprehension section of TestSMART™.)

Comprehension: This section of *TestSMART™* includes—

- 17 reading passages, which include nonfiction, fiction, and poetry selections
- multiple-choice and open-ended questions for each passage
- tag-lines that identify the skill(s) addressed in each question

Reading skills addressed in this section include—

- determining the meaning of words *(root words, context clues, multiple-meaning words, synonyms/antonyms)*
- identifying supporting ideas *(facts/details, sequential order, written directions, setting)*

- summarizing written texts *(main idea, summary of major ideas/themes/ procedures)*
- perceiving relationships and recognizing outcomes *(cause/effect, predictions, similarities/differences)*
- analyzing information to make inferences and generalizations *(inferences, interpretations/ conclusions, generalizations, character analysis)*
- recognizing points of view, propaganda, and statements of fact/opinion *(fact/opinion, author's purpose)*
- reading, analyzing, and interpreting literature *(genre identification, genre characteristics, literary elements, figurative language)*

Study Skills: This section of *TestSMART™* includes 13 practice exercises that focus on identifying and using sources of different types of information (graphic sources, parts of a book, dictionary skills). Specific skills addressed in this section include—

- using the table of contents in a book (Practices 1–2)
- using an index in a book (Practices 3–4)
- identifying appropriate sources of information (Practice 5)
- understanding the title page of a book (Practice 6)
- using a library card catalog (Practices 7–8)
- interpreting graphs (Practices 9–10)
- recognizing and using dictionary skills (Practices 11–12)
- interpreting a map (Practice 13)

5

Master Skills List/Correlation Chart:
The reading skills addressed in *TestSMART™* are based on the reading standards and/or test specifications from several different states. No two states have identical wordings for their skills lists, but there are strong similarities from one state's list to another. Of course, the skills needed for effective reading do not change from one place to another. The Master Skills List for Reading (page 9) represents a synthesis of the reading skills emphasized in various states. Teachers who use this book will recognize the skills that are stressed, even though the wording of a few objectives may vary slightly from that found in their own state's test specifications. The Master Skills Correlation Chart (page 10) offers a place to identify the skills common to both *TestSMART™* and a specific state competency test.

Vocabulary List: A list of vocabulary words appears on page 127. This list includes many of the words tested in the vocabulary section of this book and in questions that accompany some of the passages. Teachers and students can use this list to create—

- word games
- word walls
- writing activities
- "word-of-the-day" activities
- synonym/antonym charts
- word webs
- analogies
- … and more

A word of caution: In general, teachers should not ask students to memorize the words and their meanings. While some tests ask students to simply "know" the meaning of selected vocabulary words,

the majority of tests emphasize using structural cues and context clues to determine the meaning of unfamiliar words encountered during reading.

Answer Keys: Complete answer keys for multiple-choice questions appear on pages 118-120.

Scoring Guidelines and Rubrics: The scoring guidelines and sample rubrics on pages 121-126 provide important information for evaluating responses to open-ended questions. (*Note: If a state's assessment does not include open-ended questions, teachers may use the open-ended items in TestSMART™ as appropriate for their students.*) The scoring guidelines indicate the expected contents of successful responses. For example, if an open-ended question asks students to create a new title for a passage and give reasons for their answer, the scoring guideline for that question suggests specific points that students should include in the answer.

The sample rubrics allow teachers to rate the overall effectiveness and thoroughness of an answer. Once again, consider the example of creating a new title for a passage and supporting the answer with specific reasons. The corresponding rubric for that question indicates the number and quality of the reasons necessary to earn a score of "4" (for an effective, complete response) or a score of "1" (for an ineffective, incomplete response).

How to Use This Book

Effective Test Preparation: What is the most effective way to prepare students for any reading competency test? Experienced educators know that the best test preparation includes three critical components—

- a strong curriculum that includes the content and skills to be tested
- effective and varied instructional methods that allow students to learn content and skills in many different ways
- targeted practice that familiarizes students with the specific content and format of the test they will take

Obviously, a strong curriculum and effective, varied instructional methods provide the foundation for all appropriate test preparation. Contrary to what some might believe, merely "teaching the test" performs a great disservice to students. Students must acquire knowledge, practice skills, and have specific educational experiences which can never be included on tests limited by time and in scope. For this reason, books like *TestSMART*™ should **never** become the heart of the curriculum or a replacement for strong instructional methods.

Targeted Practice: *TestSMART*™ does, however, address the final element of effective test preparation (targeted test practice) in the following ways—

- *TestSMART*™ familiarizes students with the content usually included in competency tests.
- *TestSMART*™ familiarizes students with the general format of such tests.

When students become familiar with both the content and the format of a test, they know what to expect on the actual test. This, in turn, improves their chances for success.

Using *TestSMART*™: Used as part of the regular curriculum, *TestSMART*™ allows teachers to—

- pretest skills needed for the actual test students will take
- determine students' areas of strength and/or weakness
- provide meaningful test-taking practice for students
- ease students' test anxiety
- communicate test expectations and content to parents

Other Suggestions for Instruction: *TestSMART*™ can serve as a springboard for other effective instructional activities that help with test preparation.

Group Work: Teacher and students work through selected practice exercises together, noting the kinds of questions and the range of answer choices. They discuss common errors for each kind of question and strategies for avoiding these errors.

Predicting Answers: Students predict the correct answer before reading the given answer choices. This encourages students to think through the question rather than focus on finding the right answer. Students then read the given answer choices and determine which one, if any, matches the answer they have given.

Developing Test Questions: Once students become familiar with the format of test questions, they develop "test-type" questions for other assigned reading (e.g., science, social studies).

Vocabulary Development: Teacher and students foster vocabulary development in all subject areas through the use of word walls, word webs, word games, synonym/antonym charts, analogies, word categories, "word-of-the-day" activities, etc.

Two-Sentence Recaps: Students regularly summarize what they have read in one or two sentences. For fiction, students use the basic elements (setting, characters, problem, solution) to guide their summaries. For nonfiction, students use the journalist's questions (who, what, where, when, why) for the same purpose. The teacher may also list 3–5 key words from a reading selection and direct students to write a one- to two-sentence summary that includes the given words.

Generalizations: After students read a selection, the teacher states a generalization based on the reading, and students provide specific facts and details to support the generalization; or the teacher provides specifics from the selection, and students state the generalization.

Master Skills List

I. Determine the meaning of words in written texts
    A. Use root words and other structural cues to recognize new words
    B. Use context clues to determine word meaning
    C. Recognize correct meaning of words with multiple meanings
    D. Demonstrate knowledge of synonyms and antonyms

II. Identify supporting ideas
    A. Identify relevant facts and details
    B. Sequence events in chronological order (e.g., story events, steps in process)
    C. Follow written directions
    D. Identify the importance of setting to a story's meaning

III. Summarize a variety of written texts
    A. Determine the main idea or essential message of a text
    B. Summarize the major ideas, themes, or procedures of a text

IV. Perceive relationships and recognize outcomes
    A. Identify cause and effect relationships in a text
    B. Make and verify predictions with information from text
    C. Identify similarities and differences in text(s) (e.g., topics, characters)

V. Analyze information in order to make inferences and generalizations
    A. Make and explain inferences (e.g., main idea, conclusion, moral, cause/effect)
    B. Support interpretations/conclusions with information from a text
    C. Make generalizations based on information from a text
    D. Analyze characters (e.g., traits, feelings, relationships) from a story

VI. Recognize points of view, propaganda, and statements of fact and opinion
    A. Distinguish fact from opinion in a text
    B. Identify the author's purpose

VII. Read, analyze, and interpret literature
    A. Identify genres of fiction, nonfiction, and poetry
    B. Identify characteristics representative of a given genre
    C. Identify important literary elements (e.g., theme, plot, character) in a text
    D. Recognize/interpret figurative language (e.g., simile, metaphor)

VIII. Identify and use sources of different types of information
    A. Use and interpret graphic sources of information (e.g., charts, graphs)
    B. Use reference resources and the parts of a book (e.g., index) to locate information
    C. Recognize and use dictionary skills

Master Skills Correlation Chart

Use this chart to identify the *TestSMART*™ skills included on a specific state competency test. Place a check mark next to those skills common to both.

I.	**Determine the meaning of words in written texts**	
	A. Use root words and other structural cues to recognize new words	
	B. Use context clues to determine word meaning	
	C. Recognize correct meaning of words with multiple meanings	
	D. Demonstrate knowledge of synonyms and antonyms	
II.	**Identify supporting ideas**	
	A. Identify relevant facts and details	
	B. Sequence events in chronological order	
	C. Follow written directions	
	D. Identify the importance of setting to a story's meaning	
III.	**Summarize a variety of written texts**	
	A. Determine the main idea or essential message of a text	
	B. Summarize the major ideas, themes, or procedures of a text	
IV.	**Perceive relationships and recognize outcomes**	
	A. Identify cause and effect relationships in a text	
	B. Make and verify predictions with information from text	
	C. Identify similarities and differences in text(s)	
V.	**Analyze information in order to make inferences and generalizations**	
	A. Make and explain inferences	
	B. Support interpretations/conclusions with information from a text	
	C. Make generalizations based on information from a text	
	D. Analyze characters from a story	
VI.	**Recognize points of view, propaganda, and statements of fact and opinion**	
	A. Distinguish fact from opinion in a text	
	B. Identify the author's purpose	
VII.	**Read, analyze, and interpret literature**	
	A. Identify genres of fiction, nonfiction, and poetry	
	B. Identify characteristics representative of a given genre	
	C. Identify important literary elements in a text	
	D. Recognize/interpret figurative language	
VIII.	**Identify and use sources of different types of information**	
	A. Use and interpret graphic sources of information	
	B. Use reference resources and the parts of a book to locate information	
	C. Recognize and use dictionary skills	

Vocabulary

I. Determine the meaning of words in written texts

    B. Use context clues to determine word meaning

    C. Recognize correct meaning of words with multiple meanings

    D. Demonstrate knowledge of synonyms and antonyms

Practice 1: Synonyms

Directions: Read the following phrases. Find the word that has the same or about the same meaning as the bolded word. On your answer sheet, darken the circle for the correct word.

1. **conquer** your fears

   A protect
   B extend
   C compare
   D overcome

2. **exchange** the gift

   A remove
   B trade
   C purchase
   D steal

3. a lovely **melody**

   A answer
   B sight
   C tune
   D memory

4. a **responsible** student

   A likeable
   B dependable
   C removable
   D remarkable

5. a strong **odor**

   A smell
   B meaning
   C sense
   D excuse

6. **conduct** the orchestra

   A reduce
   B expand
   C question
   D direct

7. the team's **banner**

   A boss
   B victory
   C flag
   D uniform

8. a **delightful** program

   A terrible
   B wonderful
   C careful
   D failed

9. **witness** a crime

   A stop
   B see
   C report
   D arrest

10. **educate** the students

    A correct
    B remember
    C excuse
    D teach

Practice 2: Synonyms

Directions: Read the following phrases. Find the word that has the same or about the same meaning as the bolded word. On your answer sheet, darken the circle for the correct word.

1. the **regular** time for dinner

   A past
   B secret
   C normal
   D easy

2. looking **glum**

   A sad
   B angry
   C upset
   D away

3. the king's **cloak**

   A crown
   B castle
   C robe
   D power

4. **ripples** in the water

   A stones
   B pictures
   C waves
   D plants

5. a school **zone**

   A area
   B building
   C grounds
   D hallway

6. a dance **couple**

   A teacher
   B pair
   C floor
   D plan

7. **spare** tire

   A flat
   B usual
   C extra
   D old

8. **accept** the offer

   A take
   B need
   C remove
   D refuse

9. **shield** from harm

   A walk
   B protect
   C excite
   D make

10. a **feeble** old man

    A famous
    B weak
    C sneaky
    D scary

Practice 3: Synonyms

Directions: Read the following phrases. Find the word that has the same or about the same meaning as the bolded word. On your answer sheet, darken the circle for the correct word.

1. a simple **verse**

   A word
   B time
   C person
   D poem

2. the **vast** ocean

   A salty
   B tiny
   C huge
   D faraway

3. **scale** a mountain

   A bury
   B weigh
   C climb
   D protect

4. a **cluster** of grapes

   A vine
   B bowl
   C fence
   D group

5. **convince** your parents

   A persuade
   B answer
   C ask
   D ignore

6. **gobble** the food

   A swallow
   B produce
   C eat
   D move

7. the deer's **antler**

   A path
   B head
   C location
   D horn

8. **hail** a taxi

   A follow
   B ride
   C signal
   D need

9. the **slope** of the road

   A length
   B slant
   C side
   D direction

10. the **ideal** setting

    A missing
    B ugly
    C handmade
    D perfect

Practice 4: Antonyms

Directions: Read the following phrases. Find the word that has the opposite meaning of the bolded word. On your answer sheet, darken the circle for the correct word.

1. the mountain **peak**

   A rocks
   B siding
   C bottom
   D losing

2. the **exciting** story

   A terrific
   B long
   C final
   D boring

3. the **probable** result

   A unlikely
   B usual
   C daily
   D terrible

4. the **modest** actor

   A talented
   B famous
   C proud
   D noted

5. **preserve** the neighborhood

   A move
   B destroy
   C choose
   D save

6. **respect** your parents

   A need
   B dishonor
   C convince
   D flatter

7. wearing **similar** shoes

   A used
   B dirty
   C borrowed
   D different

8. **scaring** the children

   A refusing
   B comforting
   C accusing
   D remembering

9. **sturdy** buildings

   A firm
   B empty
   C small
   D weak

10. **conduct** the lesson

    A follow
    B learn
    C direct
    D forget

Practice 5: Antonyms

Directions: Read the following phrases. Find the word that has the opposite meaning of the bolded word. On your answer sheet, darken the circle for the correct word.

1. **delightful** weather

   A ideal
   B stormy
   C sunny
   D gentle

2. **arrest** the robber

   A jail
   B question
   C release
   D escape

3. feeling **affection** for her

   A liking
   B hatred
   C attention
   D distrust

4. perfect **harmony**

   A singing
   B placement
   C friendship
   D disagreement

5. **protect** the animals

   A reserve
   B change
   C harm
   D handle

6. a serious **quarrel**

   A argument
   B agreement
   C event
   D situation

7. **scorn** your enemies

   A ignore
   B admire
   C remove
   D escape

8. a **shabby** dress

   A fancy
   B ragged
   C bought
   D similar

9. **support** your friends

   A assist
   B find
   C change
   D desert

10. **excuse** the other person

    A select
    B locate
    C question
    D blame

Practice 6: Antonyms

Directions: Read the following phrases. Find the word that has the opposite meaning of the bolded word. On your answer sheet, darken the circle for the correct word.

1. locate the **exit**

   A window
   B entry
   C find
   D placement

2. **limber** movements

   A simple
   B strange
   C stiff
   D strong

3. the brave **conqueror**

   A general
   B leader
   C loser
   D fighter

4. **exchange** the presents

   A trade
   B keep
   C send
   D suggest

5. the **adventurous** child

   A brave
   B silly
   C lost
   D frightened

6. showing real **cleverness**

   A stupidity
   B understanding
   C beauty
   D education

7. **loafing** in the garden

   A resting
   B planting
   C working
   D looking

8. **scamper** away

   A hurry
   B turn
   C crawl
   D skip

9. **gentlemanly** behavior

   A kind
   B rude
   C different
   D friendly

10. to act **humbly**

    A softly
    B frightened
    C bravely
    D proudly

17

Practice 7: Context Clues

Directions: Read the following sentences. Then choose the best word to fit in the blank. On your answer sheet, darken the circle for the correct word.

1. I thought the boys were twins because they look so _____ .

   A handsome
   B active
   C similar
   D close

2. The children had a _____ about who would go first in the game.

   A situation
   B quarrel
   C program
   D need

3. Jody wants to _____ her birthday at the Pizza Pantry.

   A receive
   B decide
   C delight
   D celebrate

4. I cannot understand when you _____ your words.

   A approach
   B preserve
   C mumble
   D cluster

5. Celine was the _____ because she won every game.

   A player
   B champion
   C student
   D glider

6. The mailman left a _____ at our home.

   A parcel
   B program
   C regular
   D product

7. I watched the squirrel _____ quickly across the grass.

   A crawl
   B perform
   C climb
   D scamper

8. My grandmother asked me to put the sheets in the _____ closet.

   A lowest
   B linen
   C kitchen
   D final

Practice 8: Context Clues

Directions: Read the following sentences. Then choose the best word to fit in the blank. On your answer sheet, darken the circle for the correct word.

1. They hired a _____ to solve the case.

   A mayor
   B detective
   C gentleman
   D planner

2. Tony was excited about the party. It was hard for him to be

   _____ .

   A particular
   B going
   C patient
   D important

3. If the treehouse is not _____ , it may fall apart.

   A enjoyable
   B different
   C sturdy
   D comforting

4. To be safe, you should never _____ a stray dog or cat.

   A approach
   B escape
   C argue
   D remember

5. I remember the words to the song, but I do not know the _____ .

   A action
   B singing
   C manner
   D melody

6. The _____ building had broken windows and a leaky roof.

   A silent
   B delightful
   C shabby
   D perfect

7. David wants to study the _____ of ants.

   A house
   B colony
   C clump
   D scale

8. The _____ magazine had pictures of beautiful dresses and shoes.

   A cloth
   B fashion
   C reading
   D finish

Practice 9: Context Clues

Directions: Read the following sentences. Then choose the best word to fit in the blank. On your answer sheet, darken the circle for the correct word.

1. Tony always _____ about things he doesn't like.

   A convinces
   B requires
   C defends
   D complains

2. My boots _____ my feet from the water and mud.

   A protected
   B covered
   C polished
   D splashed

3. The store clerk put the money in the _____ .

   A counter
   B preserve
   C register
   D channel

4. The teacher gave a _____ when she wanted the children to sit down.

   A situation
   B symbol
   C signal
   D speck

5. There was a _____ of dirt on the white tablecloth.

   A dust
   B speck
   C canal
   D basin

6. I want to learn how to _____ so I can make a sweater.

   A cloak
   B knit
   C lash
   D ripple

7. The teacher asked Sean to _____ our class at the meeting.

   A require
   B exchange
   C produce
   D represent

8. Bobby was afraid to ski down the mountain _____ .

   A scale
   B slope
   C shield
   D support

20

Practice 10: Multiple-Meaning Words

Directions: Read each question. Find the word that fits both bolded meanings. On your answer sheet, darken the circle for the correct word.

1. Which word means **speedy** and **to go without food**?

   A quick
   B diet
   C fast
   D digest

2. Which word means **a herd of cattle** and **did drive**?

   A crowd
   B flocked
   C drove
   D gathering

3. Which word means **ice that falls like rain** and **a shout of welcome**?

   A drop
   B hail
   C greet
   D fall

4. Which word means **a place for learning** and **a group of fish**?

   A pond
   B class
   C net
   D school

5. Which word means **a cloth belt** and **a part of a window**?

   A sash
   B cord
   C pane
   D sill

6. Which word means **ground** and **to make dirty**?

   A earth
   B grime
   C mess
   D soil

7. Which word means **a small building** and **to get rid of**?

   A hut
   B shed
   C rid
   D home

8. Which word means **to growl** and **a tangle**?

   A bark
   B snap
   C mess
   D snarl

Practice 11: Multiple-Meaning Words

Directions: Read each pair of sentences. Find the word that completes both sentences. On your answer sheet, darken the circle for the correct word.

1. The climber _____ the mountain.

   The girl practiced _____ on the piano.

   A notes
   B climbs
   C actions
   D scales

2. Put your dirty dishes in the _____ .

   Will the boat _____ in the water?

   A sink
   B bowl
   C sail
   D place

3. How do you _____ your hair?

   I like your writing _____ .

   A line
   B style
   C creation
   D fix

4. The pitcher walked onto the baseball _____ .

   She bought the _____ for a ring.

   A field
   B box
   C diamond
   D stadium

5. He bought some black _____ for his shoes.

   My mother asked me to _____ her car.

   A laces
   B boxes
   C polish
   D wash

6. Did your parents _____ to vote?

   The clerk put the money in the _____ .

   A drawer
   B sign
   C book
   D register

Practice 12: Multiple-Meaning Words

Directions: Read each pair of sentences. Find the word that completes both sentences. On your answer sheet, darken the circle for the correct word.

1. The next _____ stepped up to the plate.

   The cake _____ was too sweet.

   A player
   B mix
   C hitter
   D batter

2. The bird splashed water with its _____ .

   The food _____ was too high.

   A head
   B tab
   C bill
   D beak

3. There was one pork _____ left in the pan.

   Who will _____ down the tree?

   A steak
   B chop
   C cut
   D slice

4. The _____ asked the king for more land.

   I could not _____ all the people.

   A knight
   B number
   C count
   D find

5. I _____ sick all day.

   She covered the board with red _____ .

   A felt
   B seemed
   C cloth
   D got

6. Grandpa planted the seeds in the _____ .

   My father bought one pound of _____ meat.

   A soil
   B ground
   C garden
   D fresh

Notes

Comprehension

I. Determine the meaning of words in written texts

A. Use root words and other structural cues to recognize new words
B. Use context clues to determine word meaning
C. Recognize correct meaning of words with multiple meanings
D. Demonstrate knowledge of synonyms and antonyms

II. Identify supporting ideas

A. Identify relevant facts and details
B. Sequence events in chronological order
C. Follow written directions
D. Identify the importance of setting to a story's meaning

III. Summarize a variety of written texts

A. Determine the main idea or essential message of a text
B. Summarize the major ideas, themes, or procedures in a text

IV. Perceive relationships and recognize outcomes

A. Identify cause and effect relationships in a text
B. Make and verify predictions with information from a text
C. Identify similarities and differences in text(s)

V. Analyze information in order to make inferences and generalizations

A. Make and explain inferences
B. Support interpretations/conclusions with information from a text
C. Make generalizations based on information from a text
D. Analyze characters from a story

VI. Recognize points of view, propaganda, and statements of fact and opinion

A. Distinguish fact from opinion in a text
B. Identify the author's purpose

VII. Determine the meaning of words in written texts

A. Identify genres of fiction, nonfiction, and poetry
B. Identify characteristics representative of a given genre
C. Identify important literary elements in a text

1: The Safe Way to Fly a Kite

Have you ever flown a kite? Kite-flying is a great way to spend a breezy day. It's always fun to watch a colorful kite **soar** and dive in the sky.

Kite-flying is **enjoyable**, but it can also be dangerous. You should know and obey many safety rules for flying a kite. Do you know what these rules are?

Safety Rules for Kite-Flying

• Never use a kite made from any kind of metal. A kite should not have any wire or string with metal pieces. Use kites made with plastic, wood, or paper parts.

• Use string that is clean and dry. Cotton string is the best.

• Never fly a kite if it is raining or storming. Lightning could strike the kite and injure you.

• Always fly a kite in an open area. A large field is a good place for kite-flying.

• Fly your kite far away from electric lines and towers. If a kite touches a power **line** or tower, it could **conduct** electricity to your body. Of course, this is very dangerous. You could suffer many serious injuries.

• Never climb an electric pole or tower to get your kite. Again, you do not want to come near electricity. You also could fall from the pole or tower and injure yourself. If your kite lands on a pole or in its wires, leave your kite there. You should call your local power company to report the problem.

• Fly a kite away from roads and streets. This is important for both you and drivers on the road. You do not want a kite to fall on passing **motorists**. This could scare them. It is also dangerous for you to **retrieve** a fallen kite from a busy street or road.

It is important to follow these rules when you fly a kite. You want to have fun. You want to be safe, too!

Synonyms/Antonyms (I.D)

1. Which word means about the same thing as **soar**?

   A Spend
   B Dive
   C Fly
   D Kite

Structural Cues (I.A)

2. What is the root of the word **enjoyable**?

   A Able
   B Joy
   C Enter
   D Enjoying

Context Clues (I.B)

3. What does the word **conduct** mean in this passage?

    A Take over
    B Guide
    C Show
    D Find

Multiple Meanings (I.C)

4. What does the word **line** mean in this passage?

    A Space between to points
    B Pencil drawing
    C Wire
    D A group of words

Structural Cues (I.A)

5. In which word do the letters *ist* mean the same as in **motorist**?

    A Fist
    B Scientist
    C Listen
    D Wrist

Context Clues (I.B)

6. What does the word **retrieve** mean?

    A To get back
    B Lose
    C Drop
    D Scare away

Facts/Details (II.A)

7. Which of the following is the best kind of string for a kite?

    A Wire
    B Metal
    C Cotton
    D Plastic

Follow Directions (II.C)

8. What should you do if your kite lands on power lines?

    A Climb carefully and get the kite
    B Move to an open area
    C Ask a driver to help you
    D Leave the kite and report the problem to the power company

Follow Directions (II.C)

9. To be safe, you should fly your kite—

    A near streets and roads
    B in a large, open area
    C close to local power lines
    D on the school grounds

Summarize Ideas/Themes (III.B)

10. Which is the best summary of this passage?

A Kite-flying is a great way to spend a breezy day.

B Kites can be made of many different materials like wood, plastic, and paper.

C There are important safety rules to follow when you fly a kite.

D You should fly a kite away from power lines and roads.

Cause/Effect (IV.A)

11. You should not fly a kite in the rain or a storm because—

A your kite could get wet

B lightning could injure you

C you will be scared

D drivers will not see you

Fact/Opinion (VI.A)

12. Which is a FACT in this passage?

A Kites should not have metal parts.

B Kite-flying is a great way to spend a breezy day.

C Kite-flying is enjoyable.

D Plastic is the best material for a kite.

Inferences (V.A)

13. Which of the following does the author seem to believe?

A Kite-flying is too dangerous for people to do.

B Kite-flying is the most enjoyable hobby for children.

C Power companies do not want people to fly kites.

D People who fly kites must be very careful.

Identify Genres (VII.A); Genre Characteristics (VII.B)

14. Is this passage fiction, nonfiction, or poetry? How do you know? Use information from the passage in your answer.

_____

_____

_____

_____

_____

_____

_____

_____

_____

_____

_____

_____

_____

2: What Do the Months Bring?

*Words to know before you read
this passage:*

dams (female animals)
gillyflowers (carnation flowers)

What do the months bring?

January brings the snow,
    Makes our feet and fingers glow.
February brings the rain,
    Thaws the frozen lake again.
March brings breezes loud and shrill,
    Stirs the dancing daffodil.

April brings the primrose sweet,
    Scatters daisies at our feet.
May brings **flocks** of pretty lambs,
    Skipping by their **fleecy** dams.
June brings tulips, lilies, roses,
    Fills the children's hands with **posies**.

Hot July brings cooling showers,
    Apricots and gillyflowers.
August brings the **sheaves** of corn,
    Then the harvest home is borne.
Warm September brings the fruit,
    Sportsmen then begin to shoot.

Fresh October brings the pheasant,
    Then to gather nuts is pleasant.
Dull November brings the blast,
    Then the leaves are whirling fast.
Chill December brings the sleet,
    Blazing fire and Christmas treat.

Context Clues (I.B)
1. In this passage, the word **flocks**
means—

A pictures
B groups
C boxes
D lands

Context Clues (I.B)
2. The word **fleecy** means—

A unhappy
B scared
C woolly
D mean

Synonyms/Antonyms (I.D)
3. Which word means about the
same thing as **sheaves**?

A Pans
B Planting
C Stems
D Pictures

Context Clues (I.B)
4. What does the word **posies** mean?

A Pieces of rock
B Lambs
C Cool showers
D Bunches of flowers

Synonyms/Antonyms (I.D)

5. Which word means about the same thing as **sportsmen**?

A Hunters
B Bakers
C Hikers
D Dancers

Facts/Details (II.A)

6. In which month do the tulips and roses bloom?

A March
B April
C June
D July

Sequential Order (II.B)

7. Which happens first during the year?

A Sportsmen begin to shoot.
B Pretty lambs skip.
C Rain thaws the frozen lake.
D There are cooling showers.

Main Idea (III.A)

8. This passage is mostly about—

A changes that happen during each month of the year
B why December is the best month of the year
C how lambs play with each other
D the different kinds of flowers that bloom each month

Similarities/Differences (IV.C)

9. The months of January and December are alike because—

A flowers grow
B there are strong winds
C people gather crops
D the weather is cold

Figurative Language (VII.D)

10. In March, the breeze *stirs the dancing daffodil. Dancing daffodil* is an example of—

A a simile
B rhyme
C personification
D a character

Identify Genres (VII.A); Genre Characteristics (VII.B)

11. Is this passage fiction, nonfiction, or poetry? How do you know? Use information from the passage in your answer.

32

3: Food Named After People

Where do foods get their names?

Some foods take their names from the people who invented them. The sandwich is a common lunch food. It took its name from James Montague. Montague lived in the 1700s. He was the Fourth Earl of Sandwich. Sandwich is an area in England. Montague liked to play cards very much. One day, he was playing in a very exciting card game. It was so exciting that he didn't want to leave the table and eat his lunch. He told his servant to bring him some meat between two slices of bread. According to the story, Montague thought he discovered a **convenient** way to eat a meal. He could eat his dinner and go on with his card game at the same time! That was the beginning of the sandwich. If you like sandwiches, you can thank John Montague for his invention.

Other foods take their names from the people who liked to eat them. Do you ever eat toast for breakfast? Have you ever eaten Melba toast? Melba toast is a very thin slice of bread that has been toasted for a long time. It is very hard and dry. An accident led to the creation of Melba toast. Nellie Melba was a famous singer at a hotel in London. One day she ordered regular toast. The chef made a mistake and cut the bread much thinner than usual. When he toasted the bread, it became very **crisp** and dry. A waiter took the toast to Nellie Melba before the chef could stop him. The chef

was upset by his **blunder**. He went to apologize to Ms. Melba. To his surprise, she was eating his "mistake." She told the chef that the toast tasted wonderful. The chef began serving the thin, dark toast to other guests at the hotel. He gave the new item a very special name. He called it Melba toast. Today, you can buy Melba toast in most grocery stores.

It's fun to find out how foods got their names! Can you think of any other foods that take their name from people?

Context Clues (I.B)
1. What does the word **convenient** mean?

   A Hard
   B Silly
   C Long
   D Easy

Multiple Meanings (I.C)
2. What does the word **crisp** mean in this passage?

   A Clear
   B Sharp
   C Lively
   D Hard

Synonyms/Antonyms (I.D)
3. Which word means about the same thing as **blunder**?

   A Waiter
   B Surprise
   C Mistake
   D Hotel

Facts/Details (II.A)

4. The first sandwich was eaten at a—

A hotel

B concert

C card game

D grocery store

Sequential Order (II.B)

5. The chef served thin, dark toast to other guests—

A after Nellie said it tasted wonderful

B before he apologized to Nellie

C just before Nellie ate the toast

D before Nellie ordered toast

Summarize Ideas/Themes (III.B)

6. Which is the best summary of this passage?

A All foods get their names in many unusual ways.

B Sandwiches are very easy to eat.

C Melba toast was caused by the chef's accident.

D Some foods, like sandwiches and Melba toast, get their names from people.

Cause/Effect (IV.A)

7. John Montague asked for meat between two slices of bread because—

A his servant did not know how to make other food

B he wanted something he could eat at the card table

C his servant had to make lunch quickly

D this was his favorite lunch

Inferences (V.A)

8. When the waiter served burned toast to Nellie, how did the chef feel?

A Angry

B Proud

C Ashamed

D Surprised

Fact/Opinion (VI.A)

9. Which is an OPINION in this passage?

A It's fun to find out how foods got their names.

B John Montague was the Fourth Earl of Sandwich.

C The chef burned Nellie's toast on purpose.

D John Montague liked sandwiches better than any other food.

Fact/Opinion (VI.A)

10. Which is a FACT in this passage?

  A John Montague played cards better than anyone else.

  B Melba toast is ordered more often than other kinds of toast.

  C Sandwich is an area in England.

  D Melba toast tastes wonderful.

Generalizations (V.C)

11. After reading this passage, you could conclude that—

  A all foods have strange names

  B most foods come from mistakes

  C foods with unusual names are fun to eat

  D some foods get their names in unusual ways

Identify Genres (VII.A); Genre Characteristics (VII.B)

12. Is this passage fiction or nonfiction? Explain your answer. Use information from the passage in your answer.

Author's Purpose (VI.B)

13. Why do you think the author wrote this passage? Give reasons for your answer. You may use information from the passage in your answer.

4: Larks in the Cornfield

There once was a family of little larks who lived with their mother in a nest in a cornfield. When the corn was ripe, the mother lark watched very carefully to see if the **reapers** were coming. She knew that when they came, their sharp knives would cut down the nest and hurt the baby larks. So every day when she went out for food, the mother lark told her little ones to look and listen very closely for everything that went on. They were to tell her all they saw and heard when she came home.

One day when the mother lark came home, the little larks were very frightened.

"Oh, Mother, dear Mother," they cried. "You must move us away tonight! The farmer was in the field today, and he said, 'The corn is ready to cut. We must call in the neighbors to help.' And then he told his son to go tonight and ask all the neighbors to come and reap the corn tomorrow."

The mother lark laughed. "Don't be frightened," she said. "If he waits for his neighbors to reap the corn, we shall have plenty of time to move. Tell me what he says tomorrow."

The next night the little larks were **trembling** with fear. The moment their mother got home they all cried out, "Mother, you must surely move us tonight! The farmer came today and said, 'The corn is getting too ripe. We cannot wait for our neighbors. We must ask our **relatives** to help us.' And then he called his son and told him to ask all the uncles and cousins to come tomorrow and cut the corn. Shall we not move tonight, dear Mother?"

"Don't worry," said the mother lark. "The uncles and cousins have plenty of reaping to do for themselves. We won't move yet."

On the third night, the mother lark came home and the little larks said, "Mother, dear, the farmer came to the field today. When he looked at the corn he was very angry and he said, 'This will never do! The corn is getting too ripe. It's no use to wait for our relatives. We shall have to cut this corn ourselves.' And then he called his son and said, 'Tomorrow we will begin to cut this corn.' Shall we move tonight, dear Mother?"

"Well," said the mother lark, "that is another story. When a man begins to do his own work instead of asking someone else to do it, things get done. Come, my little ones, I will move you out tonight."

(adapted from How to Tell Stories to Children *by Sara Cone Bryant)*

Context Clues (I.B)

1. What does the word **reapers** mean?

A Knives
B Cornfields
C People who cut crops
D Members of a family

Synonyms/Antonyms (I.D)

2. Which word means about the same thing as **trembling**?

A Shaking
B Talking
C Reaping
D Asking

Context Clues (I.B.)

3. What does the word **relatives** mean in this story?

A Reapers
B Farmers
C Family members
D Larks

Sequential Order (II.B)

4. Of the following events, which happens last in the story?

A The little larks tell Mother the farmer's relatives will help him cut the corn.
B The farmer says he and his son will cut the corn themselves.
C Mother tells the little larks to listen for the reapers.
D Mother leaves the little larks in the nest.

Setting (II.D)

5. Where is the little larks' nest?

A In a barn
B In a tree
C In a cornfield
D In an open field

Cause/Effect (IV.A)

6. The farmer decides to cut the corn with his son because—

A he does not want to hurt the little larks
B the corn is getting too ripe while he waits for others to help him
C he wants the little larks to leave the cornfield as soon as possible
D his son thinks this is the best plan

Predictions (IV.B)

7. Which of the following will the little larks likely do next?

A Tell their mother they want to stay in the cornfield one more night
B Laugh and tell their mother they were playing a trick on her
C Listen to their mother and go where she tells them to go
D Move to other nests in the cornfield that are safer

Inferences (V.A)

8. Mother does not move the little larks before because she—

A thinks the little larks are too young to leave the cornfield

B knows the farmer's neighbors and relatives will not come to help him

C believes the reapers would never hurt the little larks

D does not believe the stories they tell her

Generalizations (V.C)

9. Which of the following words best describes Mother lark?

A Silly

B Careless

C Mean

D Sensible

Character Analysis (V.D)

10. The little larks want to leave the cornfield because they—

A like adventure

B are careless

C do not like where they live

D are afraid of the reapers

Figurative Language (VII.D)

11. In this story, the larks can talk. This is an example of—

A a simile

B a metaphor

C personification

D a comparison

Summarize Ideas/Themes (III.B)

12. Which of the following sentences summarizes the story's main message?

A The farmer called his son and told him to ask all the uncles and cousins to come and cut the corn.

B There once was a family of little larks who lived with their mother in a nest in a cornfield.

C Mother lark told her little ones to look and listen very closely for everything that went on.

D When a man begins to do his own work instead of asking someone else to do it, things get done.

Interpretations/Conclusions (V.B)

13. What does Mother lark mean when she says, "When a man begins to do his own work instead of asking someone else to do it, things get done"?

5: Birbal and the Six Foolish People, Part 1

The folklore of India includes many stories about two popular characters: Akbar, a great king, and his faithful servant, Birbal. This passage retells the beginning of one of their stories.

Once upon a time in India, there was a king named Akbar. He was a strong and fair king, but sometimes he had strange ideas. Then he would ask members of his **court** to do difficult things. One day, Akbar said, "Every day I see smart people all around me. For a change, I want to see some foolish people."

His faithful servant Birbal said, "I will find six foolish people."

"Fine," said Akbar, "you have one month to bring me six fools."

"Oh, I won't need one month," answered Birbal.

The next day, Birbal set out to find six foolish people. He hadn't gone far when he saw a man standing up to his knees in a mud puddle. The man's arms were stretched stiffly out from his sides. He tried to get out of mud, but he could not.

"Do you need help, sir?" Birbal asked the man.

"Oh, yes," the man answered.

"Give me your hand. I will pull you from the mud," said Birbal.

"I can't give you my hand. My wife wants a pot this big. If I give you my hand, I will not know what size pot to buy," said the man. "Just pull me out by my hair."

Birbal grabbed the man's hair and pulled him from the mud, which was as thick as molasses. Then he wrote the man's name and address on a paper and put it in his pocket. "Here is my first foolish person," Birbal said to himself. Then he continued on his search.

Before long, Birbal met a man riding a horse. The man also carried a bale of hay on his head.

"Excuse me," Birbal said to the man. "Why do you have that bale of hay on your head?"

"Oh, my horse is very old and tired. I am sure that this bale of hay is much too heavy for him to carry, so I carry it on my head," the man answered.

Birbal just shook his head as he added the man's name and address to his paper. He had found his second foolish person.

Birbal continued walking and turned down a very narrow street. Suddenly, a man **dashed** toward him. The man crashed into Birbal and knocked him down on the **pavement**.

"What is the matter with you?" screamed Birbal. "Didn't you see me walking here?"

"Oh, I am so sorry, sir, but you got in my way. If you had moved aside, I could have caught it," answered the man.

Birbal looked around, but saw nothing. "What were you trying to catch?" he asked the man.

"I had just said my evening prayers from that church over there. I was running to see how far my voice could reach. You ruined my chance, because you were in my way," the man explained.

"This is just too easy," Birbal laughed to himself. "Imagine a man chasing his own voice down the street!" He added the man's name and address to his paper and continued down the street.

Context Clues (I.B)
1. In this passage, the word **dashed** means—

    A walked slowly
    B stood still
    C jumped high
    D ran quickly

Context Clues (I.B)
2. What does the word **pavement** mean?

    A Church steps
    B Street
    C Mud
    D Floor

Multiple Meanings (I.C)
3. What does the word **court** mean in this story?

    A A king's helpers and officers
    B A place to play tennis or basketball
    C A place to hold a trial
    D To date someone

Facts/Details (II.A)
4. The first foolish man that Birbal meets is—

    A working in the king's court
    B riding a horse
    C standing in a mud puddle
    D buying a pot at the market

Sequential Order (II.B)
5. Which event happens first in the story?

    A Birbal meets a man riding a horse.
    B Akbar says he wants to see some foolish people
    C Birbal writes the man's name on a paper
    D Birbal pulls the man from a mud puddle

Setting (II.D)

6. Where does most of this part of the story happen?

A On the streets of an Indian city
B On a farm
C At Akbar's castle
D At Birbal's house

Summarize Ideas/Themes (III.B)

7. Which is the best summary of this part of the story?

A Akbar becomes a strong and fair king in India.
B A man stands in a mud puddle and cannot get out.
C Birbal meets a foolish man who carries a bale of hay on his head.
D Akbar's servant, Birbal, sets out to find six foolish people for the king.

Cause/Effect (IV.A)

8. The man on the narrow street knocks Birbal down because he—

A wants to prove he is not foolish
B does not like Birbal
C is trying to catch his voice
D is late getting to his church

Predictions (IV.B)

9. Which of the following is Birbal most likely to do in the next part of the story?

A Tell Akbar he cannot find any foolish people
B Continue looking for more foolish people
C Tell the three men that they are foolish
D Chase the foolish man who knocked him down

Character Analysis (V.D)

10. Birbal seems to think that finding six foolish people will be—

A difficult
B dangerous
C impossible
D easy

Character Analysis (V.D)

11. How does the man feel after he knocks Birbal down?

A Sorry
B Embarrassed
C Disappointed
D Foolish

Generalizations (V.C)

12. Which word best describes this part of the story?

A Sad
B Scary
C Evil
D Funny

Figurative Language (VII.D)

13. In the story, the mud is *as thick as molasses*. *As thick as molasses* is an example of a—

A metaphor

B conclusion

C simile

D plot

Predictions (IV.B)

14. What do you think will happen in the next part of the story? Write your prediction below. Explain why you think this event will happen.

Sequential Order (II.B)

15. Think about the important events in this part of the story. List at least three important story events in the correct order.

_____

_____

_____

_____

_____

_____

_____

_____

_____

_____

_____

_____

_____

6: Birbal and the Six Foolish People, Part 2

This passage concludes the story of Birbal's search for six foolish people.

Birbal had been out for several hours. It was now dark, and the street lights burned brightly. In the distance, Birbal saw a man crawling on the ground under one of the street lights. He was obviously looking for something.

"Sir, did you lose something?" Birbal asked as he **approached** the man.

"Oh, my, yes! I have lost my diamond ring!" cried the man.

"Did you lose it right here?" asked Birbal.

"Oh, no. I lost it over there," the man said as he pointed to a park across the street. "But it is dark over there. It is easier to look for it in the bright light."

Birbal could not believe how foolish this man was. He lost his ring in a park, but he looked for it under a street light. Birbal could not believe his good **fortune** to find a fourth foolish person. He added the man's name and address to his list. Now it was very dark, indeed. Birbal decided to go home and rest. He would take his list to Akbar in the morning.

The next morning Birbal rose early and went straight to Akbar's court.

"Have you found six foolish people, Birbal?" asked Akbar.

"Yes, your majesty!" said Birbal. "And it was much easier than I thought it would be." Then Birbal gave his list of foolish people to a messenger and told him to bring them to Akbar's court.

One by one, the foolish people arrived at Akbar's court. As each one arrived, Birbal introduced him and told the story of his foolish acts. After each story, Akbar nodded his head in **satisfaction**. Indeed, Birbal had found some very foolish people!

When Birbal had finished the introductions and stories, Akbar looked around. Something was not right.

"Birbal, you promised to bring me six foolish people. I can easily count. There are only four. You have not kept your promise," Akbar said.

"Pardon me, your majesty, but I have kept my promise. I have brought four foolish people to your court, but two more are here," Birbal smiled at Akbar.

"Then, where are they, Birbal?" demanded the king.

"We are the other two foolish people, your majesty. You are a foolish person for thinking of such an idea. And I am a foolish person for obeying you!" Birbal laughed.

Akbar looked angrily at Birbal, but the other members of the court began to laugh at Birbal's joke. They laughed and laughed. Soon the entire room was filled with their **uproar**. Akbar could not help himself. He, too, began to laugh. Birbal had pulled off a very funny **prank**!

The four other foolish people received gifts from Akbar. And Birbal was the star of the king's court for many days.

Context Clues (I.B)

1. In this story, the word **approached** means—

   A went away
   B stood still
   C went near
   D hid from

Context Clues (I.B)

2. What does the word **fortune** mean in this story?

   A Actions
   B Writing
   C Luck
   D Thought

Context Clues (I.B)

3. In this story, the word **prank** means—

   A answer
   B trick
   C laugh
   D list

Context Clues (I.B)

4. What does the word **uproar** mean in this passage?

   A Foolish people
   B King's people
   C Many gifts
   D Loud laughter

Sequential Order (II.B)

5. Which of the following happens right after Birbal introduces the four foolish men?

   A Akbar begins to laugh at the foolish men.
   B Birbal becomes the star of the king's court.
   C Akbar looks around for the two missing foolish men.
   D Birbal sends the messenger to find the last two foolish men.

Setting (II.D)

6. When does Akbar meet the foolish men that Birbal has found?

   A Late at night
   B Many days after Birbal finds them
   C The same day Birbal finds them
   D The day after Birbal finds them all

Cause/Effect (IV.A)

7. The members of Akbar's court laugh because they—

A know Akbar is angry at Birbal
B think Birbal's prank is funny
C have never met foolish people before
D want to fill the room with noise

Character Analysis (V.D)

8. Members of Akbar's court probably think that Birbal's prank is—

A clever
B foolish
C stupid
D dangerous

Character Analysis (V.D)

9. How does Birbal feel after he finds the fourth foolish person?

A Foolish
B Frightened
C Lucky
D Proud

Main Idea (III.A)

10. What could be another good title for this story? Write a new title in the space below. Then explain why you think it would be a good one for this story.

Similarities/Differences (IV.C)

11. Think about the stories "Birbal and the Six Foolish People" and "The Larks in the Cornfield." How are these stories the same? How are they different? Write your ideas on the chart below.

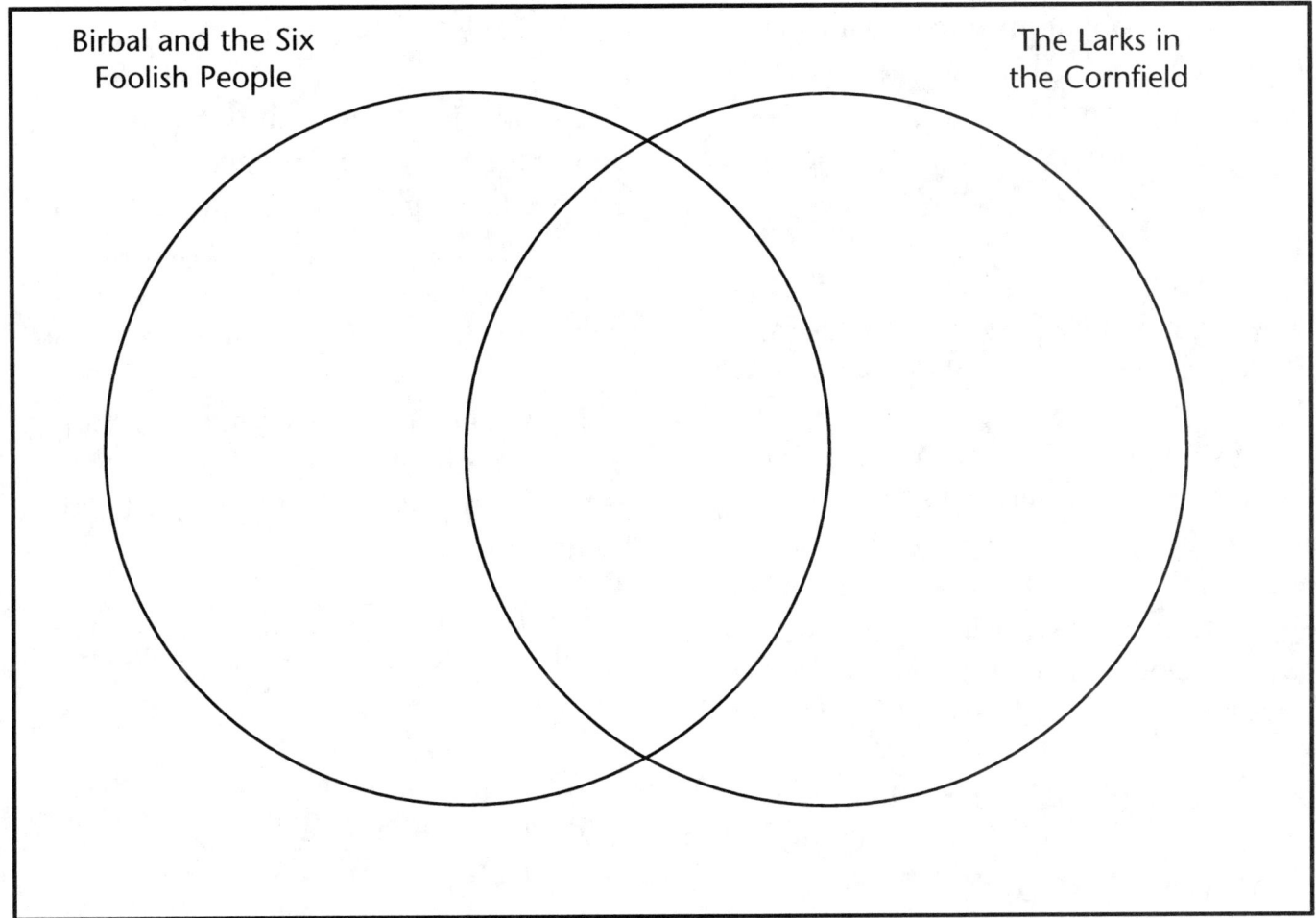

Birbal and the Six Foolish People | The Larks in the Cornfield

49

7: What Kind of Pet Is It?

In the wild, they live in **colonies**, or groups. They are lonely without one another's company. They are friendly, frisky, and furry. They are also curious and clean. They seldom bite. These little mammals are about three to four inches long—including their tails! They only weigh two or three ounces. What kind of pet is this?

If you guessed gerbils, you are right! If you want cuddly indoor companions, these critters may be just the ticket.

Housing gerbils is easy. A ten-gallon aquarium makes a fine home for two. Fill their home with several inches of **bedding**. Sawdust, wood chips, or white paper torn into small pieces are good choices. (Don't use newspaper. The ink can poison your new friends!) Do not place the aquarium in direct sunlight. Gerbils cannot live if it is too hot.

Use a small, heavy bowl for the gerbils' food. You also need a hanging water bottle. Busy gerbils **overturn** anything they can move. Replace the drinking water daily. This keeps it fresh. Change the bedding about every two weeks. At the same time, clean the aquarium with a mild soap. Then rinse it very well.

Toys will please your **perky** pets and make them more fun to watch. Give them wood to gnaw or a small piece of cloth to shred. (Never give them plastic.

They can chew through it and then swallow it.) For hiding and sleeping, gerbils like the cardboard tubes from paper towel rolls. And don't forget to give them an exercise wheel. They like to stay busy!

Gerbils don't eat meat. It is easy to supply their **vegetarian** diet. You can buy packaged gerbil food at a pet store. For a special treat, give them carrots, cheese, apples, or even wild dandelions from outside.

Now relax and enjoy your pets. Be gentle and give them the attention they need. The payoff will be their trust and friendship.

Context Clues (I.B)

1. In this passage, the word **colonies** means—

   A small mammals
   B groups of animals that live together
   C pets that live in cages
   D gerbils kept as pets

Context Clues (I.B)

2. What does the word **bedding** mean?

   A A 10-gallon aquarium
   B Old newspaper
   C Material used to make a pet's bed
   D A place to sleep

Structural Cues (I.A)

3. In which word do the letters *over* mean the same thing as in **overturn**?

    A Cover
    B Overdo
    C Mover
    D Clover

Context Clues (I.B)

4. The word **vegetarian** means—

    A containing only meat
    B containing only vegetables
    C a special treat
    D containing pet food

Synonyms/Antonyms (I.D)

5. Which word means about the same thing as **perky**?

    A Daily
    B Clean
    C Lively
    D Hungry

Facts/Details (II.A)

6. Which of the following is a good choice for a gerbil's bedding?

    A Dandelions
    B Newspaper
    C Sand
    D Wood chips

Follow Directions (II.C)

7. Since gerbils like to chew on things, you should—

    A give them only soft foods
    B use plastic toys they cannot destroy
    C clean their houses every two weeks
    D give them wood to chew

Main Idea (III.A)

8. The **fifth** paragraph in this passage is mostly about—

    A good toys for gerbils
    B why gerbils need to exercise
    C watching gerbils play
    D why gerbils like to hide

Cause/Effect (IV.A)

9. A gerbil's house should not be in direct sunlight because—

    A gerbils cannot sleep in the sunlight
    B gerbils chew more when in direct sunlight
    C too much heat can hurt gerbils
    D the gerbil's food will spoil

Fact/Opinion (VI.A)

10. Which is an OPINION in this passage?

    A Gerbils need plastic toys.

    B Gerbils are easy to care for.

    C Gerbils do not eat meat.

    D Gerbils need fresh water every day.

Author's Purpose (VI.B)

11. The author probably wrote this passage to—

    A make readers laugh

    B explain why people should not have gerbils for pets

    C describe gerbils and explain how to take care of them

    D show that gerbils are better than any other kind of pet

Identify Genres (VII.A); Genre Characteristics (VII.B)

12. Is this passage fiction or nonfiction? How do you know? Use information from the passage in your answer.

_____

_____

_____

_____

_____

_____

_____

_____

_____

Interpretations/Conclusions (V.B)

13. Would a gerbil be a good pet for you? Why or why not? Use information from the passage in your answer.

_____

_____

_____

_____

_____

_____

_____

_____

_____

_____

_____

_____

8: Be Water-Wise

We're usually disappointed when rain spoils our outdoor plans. On the other hand, we can never be sure of having enough rain. There may be months and months with no rain. Then we really have problems. Water supplies become very low. People may not have enough water to wash laundry or water crops.

A lack of rain is only one cause for low water supplies. Each year, there are more and more people living on the earth. This growth in **population** can cause water problems. More people will use more water.

Everyone uses water **carelessly**. Some use too much water on their plants. Others let water run on paved streets. Sadly, there are many ways to waste water.

You can't control the rainfall. You cannot tell people where they can live. You can use water more **wisely**. When you use water wisely, you help save it for the future. Try these simple steps and help save water.

1. Do you let the water run when you brush your teeth? You should run the water only long enough to wet your toothbrush. Fill a small cup with water. Use that water for rinsing your mouth.

2. You might help your parents water outdoor plants and flowers. Remind them to water early in the morning or late in the evening. It is cooler at these times of the day. The sun will not dry up the water before it has time to soak into the soil. Make sure that water does not run onto a sidewalk or driveway.

3. Use a bucket of water to wash the family car. Don't let water run all the time. Most of it is wasted that way.

4. Take showers instead of baths. **Limit** your shower to five minutes. Each minute that you subtract from a shower saves three to ten gallons of water.

5. Do you help with the laundry? Make sure that the washing machine has a full load each time you use it. Washing only a few items at a time wastes water.

6. If you have a dishwasher, use it wisely, too. Only run the dishwasher when it is full of dirty dishes.

These are easy steps to follow. Once you begin saving water, you may think of other ways to save even more. If you save water today, you will have the water you need in the future.

Context Clues (I.B)

1. What does the word **population** mean?

   A The number of people living in an area

   B Water supplies for people

   C Water problems caused by people

   D Lack of rain

Synonyms/Antonyms (I.D)

2. Which word means the opposite of **wisely**?

   A Carefully

   B Slowly

   C Suddenly

   D Carelessly

Structural Cues (I.A)

3. What is the root of the word **carelessly**?

   A Less

   B Care

   C Careless

   D Carefully

Multiple Meanings (I.C)

4. What is the meaning of **limit** in this passage?

   A End

   B Edge

   C Farthest away

   D Restrict

Facts/Details (II.A)

5. According to this passage, you should limit your showers to—

   A three minutes

   B five minutes

   C ten minutes

   D thirteen minutes

Follow Directions (II.C)

6. What should you do when you water your lawn?

   A Water every morning and every evening

   B Make sure the water hits the sidewalk

   C Use a bucket of water

   D Make sure the water soaks into the soil

Main Idea (III.A)

7. What is this passage mostly about?

   A Watering your lawn

   B Using water carefully

   C The lack of water in cities

   D Using dishwashwers correctly

Fact/Opinion (VI.A)

8. Which of the following is an OPINION in this passage?

   A Everyone uses water carelessly.

   B There are many causes for water problems.

   C Shorter showers use less water.

   D You should water a lawn during the early morning or late evening.

Author's Purpose (VI.B)

9. The author probably wrote this passage in order to—

   A teach people how to wash their cars

   B prove that showers are better than baths

   C explain ways that people can save water

   D explain why there will never be enough water

Generalizations (V.C)

10. How would the author probably describe most people's use of water?

   A Wise

   B Careless

   C Unnecessary

   D Easy

Cause/Effect (IV.A)

11. According to this passage, water is wasted because—

   A it has not rained in several years

   B people do not know how to save water

   C people live in cities and towns

   D people are not careful about how much water they use

Predictions (IV.B)

12. The author states that people might run out of water to wash laundry or water crops. What else might happen if people do not use water more carefully? Explain your answer. You may use information from the passage in your answer.

_____

_____

_____

_____

_____

_____

_____

_____

_____

_____

_____

_____

_____

9: Beautiful Bluebonnets

If you visit Texas in the spring, you will see fields of bluebonnets blooming beside the highways. The bluebonnet is the state flower of Texas.

The bluebonnet has had many different names. In some places people called it the wolf flower. Other people called it buffalo clover. One of its most unusual names was "el conejo." This is a Spanish **phrase** that means "the rabbit." Why did people give this name to the flower? They could see a rabbit in each tiny flower. Take a close look at a bluebonnet if you see one. Maybe you will see a rabbit, too.

Today, most people call this flower a bluebonnet. How did it earn that name? The pioneer women in Texas often wore bright hats to block the hot sun. These hats were called sunbonnets. People thought the flowers looked like the women's sunbonnets. This is how the flower earned its most popular name.

Scientists give each kind of plant a special name, too. A plant's name explains why it is **unlike** any other plant. A plant's scientific name is always in Latin, a very old language. The bluebonnet's **scientific** name is *Lupinus texensis*.

Most bluebonnet plants are from nine to twelve inches tall. The first small plants appear in early spring. They grow in small groups, or clumps, along the highways and roads. Most of the flowers look like tall towers of blue and white, but some of the flowers may be all white or pink and white. The plant's leaves and stems feel "fuzzy." The flowers have a sweet **fragrance**, or smell.

Bluebonnets are really wildflowers. This means they grow "on their own" in nature. But you can also have bluebonnets in a yard, garden, or field. It is best to plant bluebonnet seeds in the fall. Do not plant them very deep in the soil. Scatter the seeds in a place that gets lots of sun in the spring. Use a rake to spread a thin layer of dirt over the seeds. In the spring, you will have your first crop of bluebonnets.

If you want more and more bluebonnets each year, don't pick the flowers. Let them die on the plants and drop their seeds in the soil. Next year, you will have even more lovely bluebonnets to enjoy!

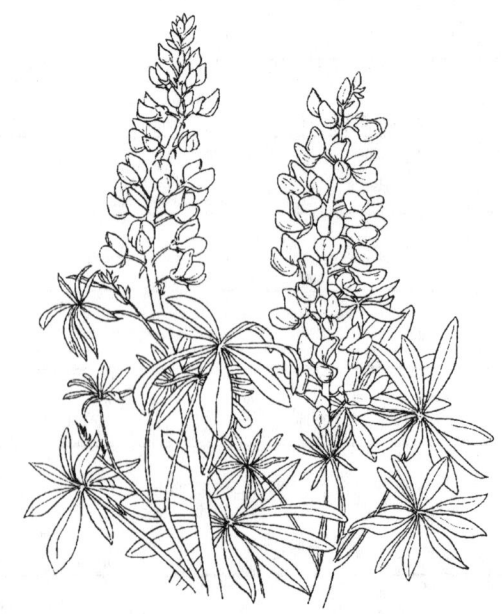

Context Clues (I.B)

1. In this passage, the word **phrase** means—

    A tiny flower
    B bluebonnet
    C group of words
    D wolf flower

Structural Cues (I.A)

2. What does the word **scientific** mean?

    A Like a flower
    B Not like science
    C Belonging to plants
    D From science

Structural Cues (I.A)

3. In this passage, what does the word **unlike** mean?

    A Special
    B Very old
    C Not the same as
    D Not in Texas

Synonyms/Antonyms (I.D)

4. Which word means about the same thing as **fragrance**?

    A Stem
    B Color
    C Soil
    D Smell

Facts/Details (II.A)

5. When should bluebonnet seeds be planted?

    A Early spring
    B June
    C Late Summer
    D Fall

Follow Directions (II.C)

6. Bluebonnet seeds should be planted—

    A deep in the soil
    B along the highway
    C in sunny places
    D away from other flowers

Main Idea (III.A)

7. The second paragraph is mostly about—

    A the correct name for a bluebonnet
    B how a flower came to be named "bluebonnet"
    C different names given to the bluebonnet
    D why the bluebonnet became the state flower of Texas

Cause/Effect (IV.A)

8. Why should you let the flowers die on the bluebonnet plants?

A So prettier flowers will grow in the spring

B So the flowers will drop their seeds in the soil

C So the flowers will be real wild flowers

D So other flowers cannot grow

Fact/Opinion (VI.A)

9. Which is an OPINION in the passage?

A Bluebonnets have a wonderful smell.

B Bluebonnets were called buffalo clover.

C Bluebonnet flowers can be pink and white.

D The bluebonnet is the state flower of Texas.

Genre Characteristics (VII.B)

10. This passage is nonfiction because it—

A tells a story about how Texas was settled by pioneer women

B uses many rhyming words to describe the bluebonnet

C presents true information about the bluebonnet

D explains why Texas chose the bluebonnet as its state flower

Interpretations/Conclusions (V.B)

11. The bluebonnet is the state flower of Texas. Why do you think Texas chose this flower? Use information from the passage in your answer.

Similarities/Differences (IV.C)

12. The author of this passage compares the bluebonnet to other things. Find at least two of these comparisons. List and explain each one.

10: My Early Home

The following passage is from the first chapter of the book Black Beauty, *by Anna Sewell. It is a story about the life of a beautiful horse.*

The first place that I can well remember was a large pleasant meadow with a pond of clear water in it. Some shady trees leaned over it, and rushes and water lilies grew at the deep end. Over the hedge on one side, we looked into a plowed field. On the other side we looked over a gate at our master's house, which stood by the roadside. At the top of the meadow was a **plantation** of fir trees, and at the bottom, a running brook overhung by a steep **bank**.

While I was young, I lived upon my mother's milk because I could not eat grass. In the day time, I ran by her side. At night, I lay down close by her. When it was hot, we stood by the pond in the shade of the trees. When it was cold, we had a nice warm shed near the plantation.

As soon as I was old enough to eat grass, my mother went out to work in the day time and came back in the evening.

There were six young colts in the meadow besides me. They were older than I was; some were nearly as large as grown-up horses. I used to run with them, and had great fun. We used to gallop all together round and round the field, as hard as we could go. Sometimes we had rather rough play, and they would bite and kick as well as gallop.

One day, when there was a good deal of kicking, my mother **whinnied** to me to come to her, and then she said:

"I want you to pay attention to what I am going to say to you. The colts that live here are very good colts, but they are cart-horse colts. Of course, they have not learned manners. You have been well-bred and well born. Your father has a great name in these parts, and your grandfather won the **cup** two years at the Newmarket races. Your grandmother had the **sweetest** temper of any horse I ever knew, and I think you have never seen me kick or bite. I hope you will grow up gentle and good, and never learn bad ways. Do your work with a good will, lift your feet up well when you trot, and never bite or kick, even in play."

I have never forgotten my mother's advice; I knew she was a wise old horse, and our master thought a great deal of her. Her name was Duchess, but he often called her Pet.

Our master was a good, kind man. He gave us good food, good lodging, and kind words. He spoke as kindly to us as he did to his own children. We were all fond of him, and my mother loved him very much. When she saw him at the gate, she would neigh with joy and trot up to him. He would pat and stroke her and say, "Well, old Pet, and how is your little Darkie?" I was a dull black, so he called me Darkie. Then he would give me a piece of bread, which was very good. Sometimes he brought a carrot for my mother. All the horses would come up to him, but I think we were his favorites. My mother always took him to the town on a market day in a little carriage.

Multiple Meanings (I.C)

1. In this passage, the word **bank** means—

A a place to keep or borrow money
B the rising ground beside a river
C a row or line of things
D to depend on

Context Clues (I.B)

2. What does the word **plantation** mean?

A Road
B River
C Bottom
D Large group

Context Clues (I.B)

3. The word **whinnied** means—

A ran
B came close
C kicked
D made soft noises

Synonyms/Antonyms (I.D)

4. Which word means about the same thing as **cup** as it is used in this passage?

A Bowl
B Race
C Award
D Glass

Structural Cues (I.A)

5. In which word do the letters *est* mean the same thing as in the word **sweetest**?

A Yesterday
B Pester
C Funniest
D Estimate

Facts/Details (II.A)

6. What food does the master bring for Darkie's mother?

A Carrots
B Bread
C Oats
D Grass

Setting (II.D)

7. When this story opens, where does Darkie live?

A In a town
B In Newmarket
C In a meadow
D In the water

Cause/Effect (IV.A)

8. Darkie's mother tells him never to bite or kick because—

A his father will be upset
B she wants him to be gentle and good
C he will run in a race soon
D their master will be angry

Inferences (V.A)

9. The master probably lets Darkie's mother take him to town because she—

A is the only horse that can pull a carriage
B trots to the fence and begs for food
C has the youngest colt
D is one of his favorite horses

Generalizations (V.C); Character Analysis (V.D)

10. From information in the story, it seems most likely that Duchess believes—

A the other colts in the meadow are stronger than her colt
B her colt comes from a better family than the other colts
C the master is scary and mean
D her colt will grow up to be a cart-horse colt

Identify Genre (VII.A)

11. This passage is part of a—

A poem
B fairy tale
C novel
D newspaper article

Figurative Language (VII.D)

12. In this passage, horses can talk to each other. This is an example of—

A a simile
B rhyme
C a metaphor
D personification

Main Idea (III.A)

13. The title of this passage is "My Early Home." What would be another good title? Explain why you think this would be a good title.

Character Analysis (V.D)

14. What do we learn about Duchess and her colt in this passage? Write a paragraph that tells about these two characters. Use information from the passage in your answer.

_____

_____

_____

_____

_____

_____

_____

_____

_____

_____

_____

_____

_____

11: Around and Around

Rain comes from the clouds that move through the sky above us. Raindrops come in all sizes. Some are big and fat. Others are only small **droplets** of water. The rain falls from the sky and flows into puddles, streams, rivers, lakes, and oceans. All the raindrops that **form** our **waterways** take a long journey to reach the earth.

After a storm or shower ends, the sun may come out. The sun's hot rays reach the puddles made by the rain. Just like a stove heats our food and water, the sun's rays warm the puddles. Soon the puddles begin to dry. The water seems to disappear, but it has only returned to the air. There it begins its journey again.

The sun's heat changes the water into a gas. When water is a gas, we usually can't see it. The gas is called water vapor. The change from water to a gas is called **evaporation**.

As the gas rises into the air, the wind takes it and other raindrops back into the sky. After a while, the water vapor forms into clouds again. If the wind is strong, the clouds move swiftly through the sky. The wind can carry one drop of rain far away. Raindrops may travel hundreds of miles. They can even travel to other countries. Sooner or later, though, the raindrops fall back to earth again.

These changes and movements are part of the water cycle. The word "cycle" really means "circle." The earth's water travels in a circle as it falls to land and then returns to the sky again.

Every drop of water travels through the water cycle. This can be a short journey. Or a single raindrop may travel all the way around the world. The next raindrop that hits your head may have been part of a faraway ocean last year.

Structural Cues (I.A)

1. What is the base word of **evaporation**?

   A Pore
   B Evaporate
   C Vapors
   D Explore

Structural Cues (I.A)

2. In this passage, what does the word **droplets** mean?

   A Large, fat raindrops
   B Streams or rivers
   C Small drops of water
   D Clouds

Antonyms/Synonyms (I.D)

3. Which word is not a synonym for **waterway**?

   A Streams
   B Rivers
   C Lakes
   D Raindrops

Multiple Meanings (I.C)

4. What does the word **form** mean in this passage?

  A Make up
  B Shape
  C Paper
  D Start

Summarize Ideas/Themes (III.B)

5. Which sentence tells what this passage is mostly about?

  A Rain comes from clouds that move through the sky.
  B Water cannot be seen when it is a gas.
  C As part of the water cycle, rain drops go through changes and travel many miles.
  D Heat from the sun changes rain drops into water vapor.

Cause/Effect (IV.A)

6. Puddles of water dry and seem to disappear because—

  A heat from the sun changes the water into a gas
  B stoves heat the water
  C all water must go through the water cycle
  D the water must travel to faraway places

Facts/Details (II.A)

7. What does the word **cycle** mean?

  A Rain
  B Upward
  C Journey
  D Circle

Genre Characteristics (VII.B)

8. This kind of passage would most likely appear in a—

  A spelling book
  B history book
  C science book
  D novel

Sequential Order (II.B)

9. This passage explains the water cycle. List the steps in the water cycle. Begin with the first step listed below. Use information from the passage in your answer.

1. Rain falls from the clouds.

_____

_____

_____

_____

_____

_____

_____

_____

_____

_____

_____

_____

_____

_____

12: Rainbow Happiness

It was raining. Molly couldn't go outside and play. She was disappointed because she had to be inside all day. She wondered what it would be like if she always had to stay inside. She thought that never seeing the sunshine or feeling a breeze would be terrible. Going outside and enjoying beautiful things each day was her favorite thing to do.

"Molly, it's time to go visit Grandma!" Molly's mother called to her. Today they were going to visit Grandma in a **nursing home**. Grandma was old. She stayed in a home with other **elderly** people. At the nursing home, Grandma got the kind of care she needed. Molly liked to visit her Grandma each week. Everyone was always happy on those special visits.

"Look! A rainbow!" Molly exclaimed as they drove. It had stopped raining. Now a beautiful rainbow arched in the sky. Molly thought again about how disappointed she was when she couldn't go outside. The beautiful rainbow was a great way to make her day happy again. She wished that Grandma could see the rainbow, too. But, she knew that Grandma had to stay inside since the ground was wet. Molly would have to describe the pretty rainbow to Grandma instead.

When they arrived at the nursing home, Molly led the family down the hall to Grandma's room. She knew exactly where it was. She visited Grandma every weekend. Grandma was happy to see the family again. They all talked and laughed for the **rest** of the afternoon. Molly was pleased to see everyone so happy.

When it was time for the family to leave, Molly saw the **disappointment** in Grandma's eyes. Molly knew that they would be back to visit next weekend, but it was still sad to leave Grandma. On the drive home, Molly looked out the window to see the rainbow, but it wasn't there anymore. She wished it could have been there to cheer her up again.

When Molly got home, she had an idea. She took out her construction paper, markers, and scissors and went to work. She worked on her project each night after school that week. She didn't rush to finish. She wanted everything to be perfect.

The weekend finally came. Molly finished her project just in time to take it to the nursing home. When she saw Grandma, she opened her bag and pulled out the surprise.

"It's a rainbow to hang in your room, Grandma. I saw one after the rainstorm last week. It cheered me up because it was so beautiful. I decided to make one for you. Now you can feel cheered up each time you see it. I made one for each of your friends, too. I hope they like them," Molly said happily.

Molly made the rainbows to make other people happy, but they made her feel great, too. It felt nice to make someone's day brighter.

Context Clues (I.B)

1. What does the word **elderly** mean?

   A Special
   B Old
   C Nice
   D Sad

Context Clues (I.B)

2. In this passage, what does the term **nursing home** mean?

   A A place to work on projects
   B A place to visit family members
   C A home for old people who need special care
   D A home without any windows

Structural Cues (I.A)

3. In which word do the letters *dis* mean the same as in **disappointment**?

   A Dish
   B Distant
   C Disk
   D Disappear

Multiple Meanings (I.C)

4. What does the word **rest** mean in this passage?

   A Something that remains
   B Stop
   C Place against something
   D Sit down

Sequential Order (II.B)

5. In this story, Molly first sees a rainbow—

   A on the way home from the nursing home
   B before she leaves for the nursing home
   C while she is visiting Grandma
   D on the way to visit Grandma

Setting (II.D)

6. Most of this story happens—

   A at Molly's school
   B in Molly's yard
   C at the nursing home
   D on a road

Main Idea (III.A)

7. This story is mostly about—

   A why Molly's grandmother is in a nursing home
   B how rainbows help make a girl and her grandmother happy
   C a little girl who does not like the rain
   D the best way to make elderly people happy

Cause/Effect (IV.A)

8. Grandma stays in a nursing home because—

A she needs special care

B all old people live in nursing homes

C her family can visit her there

D she has to stay inside all the time

Predictions (IV.B)

9. Which of the following is Molly most likely to do?

A Stay home the next time her family visits Grandma

B Take the paper rainbows when she leaves the nursing home

C Help Grandma and her friends hang the rainbows in their rooms

D Tell Grandma that she should not be sad when Molly goes home

Character Analysis (V.D)

10. When Molly gives the paper rainbow to Grandma, Grandma probably feels—

A tired

B lonely

C calm

D pleased

Interpretations/Conclusions (V.B)

11. Molly makes a rainbow for Grandma because—

A Grandma has never seen a rainbow

B Grandma asks her to make the rainbow

C she believes rainbows can make Grandma happy

D she wants to use her paper and markers

Character Analysis (V.D)

12. Think about Molly. What kind of girl does she seem to be? How would you describe her? Write a paragraph that explains what you think about Molly. Use information from the story in your answer.

Interpretations/Conclusions (V.B)

13. Write a letter to the author of this story. In the letter, tell the author what you liked about the story. Use information from the passage in your answer.

_____

_____

_____

_____

_____

_____

_____

_____

_____

_____

_____

_____

_____

_____

13: How to Wrap a Present

Have you ever wrapped a present for someone? **Wrapping** a gift so that it looks neat and pretty may seem like a hard job. However, if you gather the right materials and follow some simple steps, you can create a package that others will like.

First, gather all the items you need for wrapping a gift. For most projects you will need wrapping paper, tape, scissors, ribbon, a gift tag, and a pen or pencil. Of course, you also need the gift that you want to wrap! Wrapping the gift is easier if it is in some sort of box.

Find a clean, flat surface for wrapping the present. A table or the floor is a good place to work. Cut a piece of wrapping paper large enough to wrap around the gift. Place the paper on your work surface with the printed side down. Then, place the gift in the center of the wrapping paper.

Next, pick up the edge of the paper and wrap the paper around the package. Make sure the paper fits closely against the gift. Hold the paper there, and pick up the edge of the paper on the opposite side of the gift. Wrap it across the gift in the same way you wrapped the first side. The second edge should cross over the first edge by at least one inch so the gift box is covered. **Fasten** the second edge of paper down to the other side with two or three small pieces of tape.

Two sides of the wrapping paper should still be open and not attached to the gift. Start at one of the open sides. Fold the wrapping paper neatly against the side of the package. Then, tape the folded paper down so it will not come open. Repeat the same steps at the end that is still open and not attached to the box. Once you finish these steps, your gift should be wrapped in the paper. No part of the gift should be **visible**.

Next, you make a bow and place it on the package. Before making the bow, look at the size of the package. Large packages usually have large bows. Small packages usually have small bows. Make a bow that fits the size of your package. Then fasten the bow to the package with some tape.

Finally, make a gift tag. On the tag, write the name of the person who will be receiving the present. You also can write the name of the person who is giving the present.

Now you are ready to give the gift to some lucky person.

Structural Cues (I.A)

1. What is the root of the word **wrapping**?

   A Wrapped
   B Rapped
   C Wrapper
   D Wrap

Synonyms/Antonyms (I.D)

2. Which of the following words means the OPPOSITE of **fasten**?

   A Tape
   B Wrap
   C Open
   D Edge

Sequential Order (II.B)

3. What is the first step in wrapping a present?

   A Finding a clean, flat surface
   B Gathering all the materials
   C Cutting the paper the right size
   D Making a bow for the package

Follow Directions (II.C)

4. When you wrap the paper around the package, you should—

   A wrap it loosely around the gift
   B let part of the gift show
   C tape it to the gift box
   D wrap it closely around the gift

Main Idea (III.A)

5. What is this passage mainly about?

   A How to give presents to people
   B How to find materials for wrapping a present
   C How to wrap a present
   D How to make bows and gift tags

Interpretations/Conclusions (V.B)

6. If you follow and practice the directions in this passage, you will—

   A receive more presents
   B learn how to wrap neat and pretty packages
   C wrap packages better than any one else
   D be invited to many parties

Facts/Details (II.A)

7. Which one of the following is NOT listed in this passage as something you need for wrapping a present?

   A String
   B Scissors
   C Flat surface
   D Tape

Sequential Order (II.B)

8. What should you do right before you make the bow for the package?

   A Check how long the ribbon is
   B Make a large and small bow
   C Check the size of the package
   D Fasten the paper with tape

Identify Genres (VII.A)

9. This passage is a—

A story
B set of directions
C poem
D mystery

Author's Purpose (VI.B)

10. The author probably wrote this passage in order to—

A get presents from people
B encourage people to give each other gifts
C explain how to wrap a present
D show that wrapping a present is difficult to do

Sequential Order (II.B)

11. What are the main steps in wrapping a present? List each step on the lines below.
Number the steps in order. Use information from the passage in your answer.

_____

_____

_____

_____

_____

_____

_____

_____

_____

_____

_____

_____

_____

14: A Different Kind of Bird

Owls have a unique appearance. They have large, round heads. Their large eyes are set in the front of their heads. This gives owls an interesting "stare." People sometimes say an owl looks **wise**, or smart, because of its stare.

A layer of feathers covers an owl's body. The feathers are so thick that an owl seems to have no neck. Some owls have a ring of feathers around each eye. The rings look like eyeglasses and add to their wise look. Owls are usually not colorful birds. Most have gray, tan, or brown feathers. There are exceptions. The snowy owl lives in the Arctic region. Its feathers are white like the snow and ice where it lives.

The eagle owl is a large bird from Africa and Asia. It can be 30 inches from head to tail, have a wingspan of five to six feet, and weigh more than five pounds. Then there is the elf owl, a very small bird. It lives in some desert regions of North America and is only five inches long.

Owls hunt and kill other animals for food. They have special claws called **talons**. The talons are perfect for grabbing mice, frogs, and rabbits. Owls also have sharp beaks. With their sharp talons and beaks, owls are some of nature's best hunters.

Most owls are **nocturnal** animals. This means they are most active at night. Excellent eyesight lets owls see well in the dark. The pupils in their eyes open widely. This lets light enter the eyes so owls can see their prey in the dark.

Owls have good eyesight, but they cannot move their eyes very much. To see something to the side or behind, they must turn their entire head. They can do this easily because they have **flexible** necks. Some owls can turn their heads completely around and look behind them.

Owls may have great eyesight, but they also have excellent hearing. Feathers cover their "ears," which are large openings on each side of their head. Owls use the feathers to direct sounds into the openings. Owls can hear soft sounds coming from 75 feet away.

Large wings covered with soft feathers also help owls at night. The feathers make very little sound as owls fly, so they can fly almost silently. They can approach their prey and not be heard.

Most owls do not make nests. Some find or make holes in the ground. Others use holes they find in trees. Some even use old nests built by another kind of bird. Owls like to use the same nest year after year.

A female owl lays from 2 to 12

white, round eggs. She lays the eggs at different times, so they hatch at different rates. Usually, the female sits on the eggs, and the male brings food to her. Both the male and female protect their nests and young. They will attack any animal or person that comes too near.

The female owl stays with the tiny **owlets** for about one month after they hatch. Then they learn how to fly. Once an owlet knows how to fly, it leaves the nest and finds its own place to live and hunt.

Owls are beautiful and interesting, but they also help people. Insects and rodents are an important part of an owl's diet. Owls help farmers and ranchers because they eat these small creatures that can damage crops.

An owl's special characteristics and appearance set it apart from other birds. It's easy to understand why so many people like owls.

Context Clues (I.B)
1. In this passage, the word **wise** means—

   A smart
   B large
   C round
   D interesting

Context Clues (I.B)
2. What does the word **nocturnal** mean?

   A Having good eyesight
   B Excellent
   C Active at night
   D Open wide

Context Clues (I.B)
3. What does the word **talons** mean?

   A Hunters
   B Sharp claws
   C Special beaks
   D Food

Structural Cues (I.A)
4. The word **owlets** means—

   A female owls
   B baby owls
   C owl nests
   D male owls

Facts/Details (II.A)
5. About how long is the elf owl?

   A 6 feet
   B 5 feet
   C 30 inches
   D 5 inches

Sequential Order (II.B)

6. What happens after a young owl learns to fly?

A It stays in the nest for one more month.

B It brings food for the female to eat.

C It leaves the nest and finds its own place to live.

D It lays 2 to 12 white eggs.

Main Idea (III.A)

7. This passage is mostly about how owls—

A hunt for food

B look and act

C raise their young

D help people

Cause/Effect (IV.A)

8. The male owls bring food to the female owls because—

A female owls do not hunt

B female owls attack any animal too close to the nest

C female owls must sit on the eggs to hatch them

D male owls have sharper talons than female owls

Generalizations (V.C)

9. You can tell from the passage that people usually find owls to be—

A harmful

B helpful

C more beautiful than other birds

D more colorful than other birds

Fact/Opinion (VI.A)

10. Which is an OPINION in this passage?

A Most owls have gray, tan, or brown feathers.

B Most owls are active at night.

C Both male and female owls protect their nests and young.

D Owls are beautiful and interesting.

Author's Purpose (VI.B)

11. The author probably wrote this passage in order to—

A prove owls are better than any other birds

B explain why owls are good hunters

C describe owls' appearance and behavior

D warn people that owls can be dangerous

Identify Genre (VII.A)

12. What kind of passage is this?

    A An adventure

    B A poem

    C An informational passage

    D A mystery

Interpretations/Conclusions (V.B)

13. The title of this passage is "A Different Kind of Bird." Explain why the owl is a different kind of bird. Use information from the passage in your answer.

15: The Elves and the Shoemaker

Once upon a time, there was an honest shoemaker who was very poor. He worked as hard as he could, and still he could not earn enough to keep himself and his wife. At last there came a day when he had nothing left but one piece of leather, big enough to make one pair of shoes. He cut out the shoes, ready to stitch, and left them on the bench. Then he went to bed, trusting that he could finish the shoes on the next day and sell them.

Bright and early the next morning, the shoemaker rose and went to his workbench. There lay a pair of shoes, beautifully made, and the leather was all gone! The shoemaker looked all around, but there was no sign of anyone else. The shoemaker and his wife did not know what to make of it. The first customer who came in that day was so pleased with the beautiful shoes that he bought them. He paid so much that the shoemaker could buy enough leather for two pairs of shoes.

Happily, the shoemaker cut out the shoes. Then, since it was late, he left the pieces on the bench, ready to sew in the morning. But when the morning came, two pairs of shoes lay on the bench, most beautifully made. Again, there was no sign of anyone else. The shoemaker and his wife were at a complete loss about what was happening.

That day a customer came and bought both pairs of shoes. He paid so much for them that the shoemaker bought enough leather for four pairs of shoes. Once more, he cut out the shoes and left them on the bench. In the morning, all four pairs of shoes were made.

It went on like this until the shoemaker and his wife were very **prosperous** people, but they could not be totally happy. They could not be **satisfied** to have so much and not know whom to thank for all they had. So, one night after the shoemaker had left the pieces of leather on the bench, he and his wife hid behind a curtain and left a light in the room.

Just as the clock struck twelve, the door opened softly and two tiny elves came dancing into the room. They hopped on to the bench and began to put the pieces of leather together. They had **wee** little scissors and hammers and thread. Tap, tap, went the little hammers; stitch, stitch went the thread. The little elves worked very hard. No one ever worked as fast as they did. In almost no time, all the shoes were stitched and finished. Then the tiny elves took hold of each other's hands and danced around the shoes on the bench. They looked like two dancing dolls. The shoemaker and his wife had to work hard not to laugh aloud. When the clock struck two, the little creatures **whisked** away out the window and left the room as it was before.

The shoemaker looked at his wife and said, "How can we thank the little elves who have made us happy and prosperous?"

"I should like to make them some pretty clothes," said the wife. "The clothes they have are ragged and torn."

"I will make the shoes, if you will make the clothes," said her husband.

That very day, they set to work. The wife cut out two tiny, tiny coats of green; two teeny, teeny pairs of pants of white; and two bits of caps of bright red (for everyone knows that elves like bright colors). Her husband made two little pairs of shoes with long, pointed toes. They made the wee clothes with nice little stitches and beautiful buttons. By the next evening, they were finished.

That night the shoemaker cleaned his bench and on it, instead of leather, he laid the two sets of little elf clothes. Then, he and his wife hid behind the curtain as before.

Promptly at midnight, the little elves came in. They hopped up on the bench, but when they saw the little clothes, they laughed and danced for joy. Each one took up his little coat and pants and hat and began to put them on. Then they hopped down and began to dance and dance and dance. When the clock struck two, they danced away and out the window.

The little elves never came back. The shoemaker and his wife had just great **fortune** and never needed anyone's help again.

(adapted from How to Tell Stories to Children *by Sara Cone Bryant)*

Context Clues (I.B)

1. In this story, the word **prosperous** means—

   A poor
   B angry
   C upset
   D rich

Context Clues (I.B)

2. What does the word **satisfied** mean?

   A Pleased
   B Working
   C Rich
   D Poor

Context Clues (I.B)

3. The word **wee** means—

   A broken
   B small
   C many
   D soft

Synonyms/Antonyms (I.D)

4. Which word means about the same as the word **whisked** in this story?

A Hurried
B Fell
C Entered
D Opened

Synonyms/Antonyms (I.D)

5. Which word means about the same as the word **fortune** in this story?

A Anger
B Shoes
C Luck
D Elves

Sequential Order (II.B)

6. Which of the following happens first in this story?

A The shoemaker and his wife make clothes for the elves
B The shoemaker and his wife hide behind the curtain.
C The shoemaker cuts out one pair of shoes and leaves them on the bench.
D The shoemaker and his wife see the elves dancing in the room.

Setting (II.D)

7. Most of this story takes place—

A outside the shoemaker's window
B just outside the shoemaker's house
C behind the curtain of a stage
D inside the shoemaker's work room

Cause/Effect (IV.A)

8. The shoemaker and his wife hide behind the curtain because they—

A want to see who makes the shoes each night
B are afraid of the elves
C want to make several pairs of shoes before morning
D know the elves will find them there

Generalizations (V.C)

9. When the elves finish making the shoes, they seem to be—

A frightened
B tired
C happy
D curious

Figurative Language (VII.D)

10. When the elves danced, they *looked like two small dancing dolls*. The phrase *like two dancing dolls* is—

A personification
B a simile
C a metaphor
D rhyme

Author's Purpose (VI.B)

11. The author probably wrote this story in order to—

   A explain how elves help people

   B teach readers something about making shoes

   C entertain readers with a story

   D show how elves spend their time

Similarities/Differences (IV.C)

12. Think about the elves and the shoemaker and his wife. How are the elves like the shoemaker and his wife? How are they different? Write your ideas on the chart.

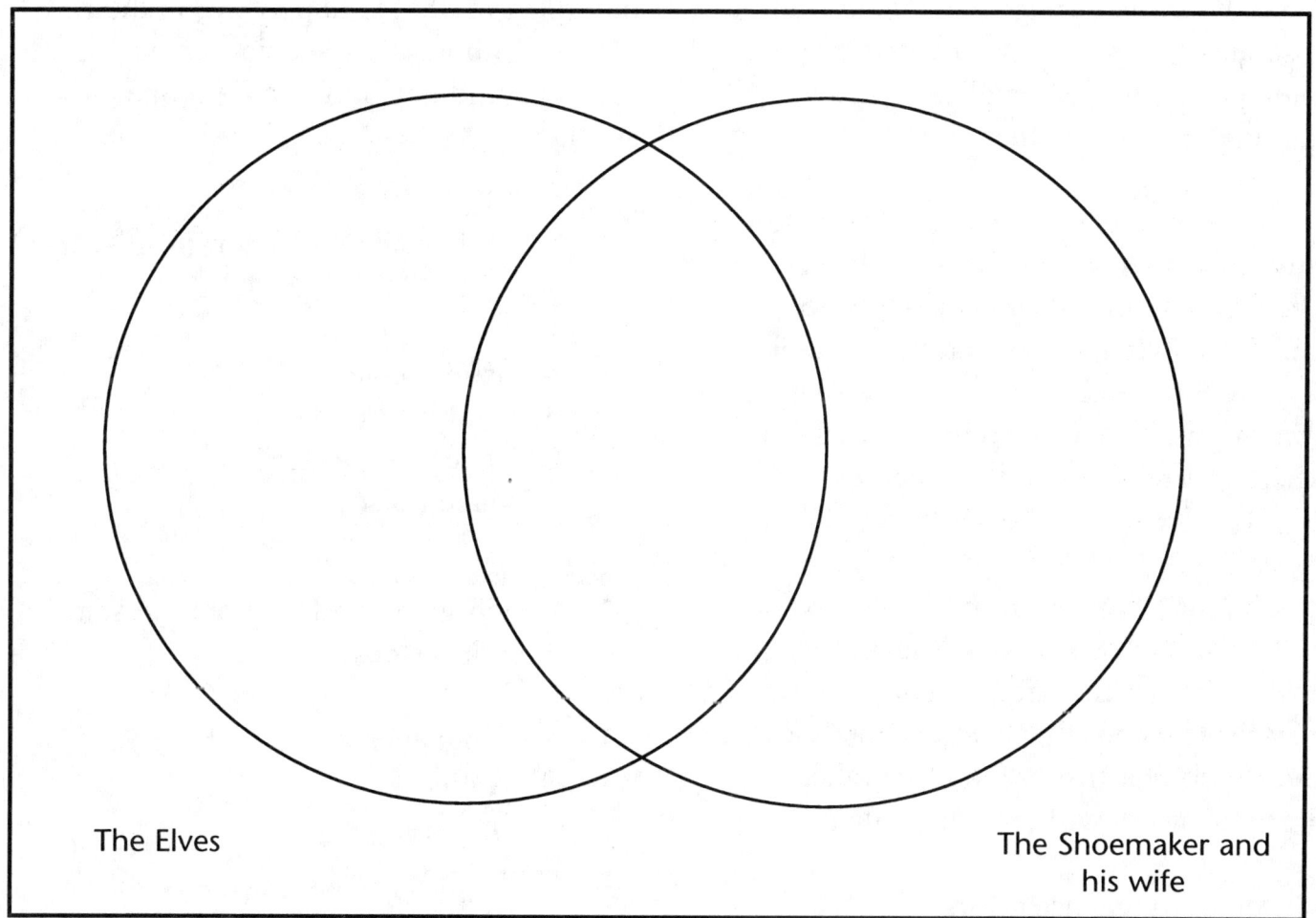

The Elves

The Shoemaker and his wife

16: Insect Languages

Did you know that insects can send messages to one another? In fact, they have many ways to **communicate**. They can warn one another of danger. They can send directions for finding food or give each other important messages.

Some insects communicate with special sounds. These sounds are not like human speech, but they do the same job. For example, crickets make chirping noises with their wings when they want to send messages to each other. On quiet summer nights, you can hear crickets "talking" to one another.

Other insects use movement to send their messages. Honey bees do dances. Their dances tell other bees where to find food. When the bees return to their hive with food, they dance in the shape of an eight. The dance tells other bees where to find food and how far away it is.

You may have seen fireflies blinking in the dark. Why do these "lightning bugs" turn on their lights? This is how they let other fireflies know where they are. When one firefly blinks, another firefly answers with a blink of its own.

Some insects use **odors** to communicate with each other. For example, some moths release an odor that helps them find one another. The moths have a good sense of smell. They can follow the odors and find the moths that are sending the message.

Ants give each other information through touch. You may have seen the way ants stop and touch one another when they meet on the ground. This is one way they "talk" to each other. It also helps explain how so many ants are able to find the same small piece of food!

Insects have many ways to let each other know what is happening in their world. Without their special languages, insects could not find and help one another.

Context Clues (I.B)

1. What does the word **communicate** mean in this passage?

   A Grow longer
   B Send information
   C Dance
   D Make noises

Synonyms/Antonyms (I.D)

2. Which word means about the same thing as **odors**?

   A Languages
   B Moths
   C Smells
   D Senses

Facts/Details (II.A)

3. How do crickets "talk" to each other?

A They make noises with their wings.

B They release an odor.

C They do a special dance.

D They touch the bees in the hive.

Main Idea (III.A)

4. What is the main idea of this passage?

A People and insects send messages in different ways.

B Dancing is one way to send a message.

C People have better ways to send information than insects.

D Insects have many ways to send messages to each other.

Fact/Opinion (VI.A)

5. Which of these is a FACT stated in this passage?

A Bees like to dance for each other.

B Crickets make the loudest noises on a quiet night.

C Some insects use movement or sound to send messages to each other.

D People can understand many of the codes that insects use.

Main Idea (III.A)

6. What is the main idea of the second paragraph in this passage?

A Crickets make loud chirping noises.

B You can hear crickets on a quite night.

C Insects can use sounds to send messages.

D Human speech is different from insect sounds.

Interpretations/Conclusions (V.B)

7. How do honey bees show other bees where food can be found?

A The bees follow each other so they can find food together.

B The bees make noises with their wings.

C The bees release an odor that tells the other bees where to find food.

D The bees make a special movement in their dance that tells the direction of the food.

Cause/Effect (IV.A)

8. Fireflies can find each other at night because they—

A make special noises

B have an unusual smell

C do a special dance

D blink their lights

Summarize Ideas (III.B); Facts/Details (II.A)

9. According to this passage, what are some of the ways that insects communicate? List and explain each way. Use information from the passage in your answer.

Similarities/Differences (IV.C)

10. What is different about the way insects communicate and the way people communicate? What is the same? Write your ideas on the chart below. Use information from the passage in your answer.

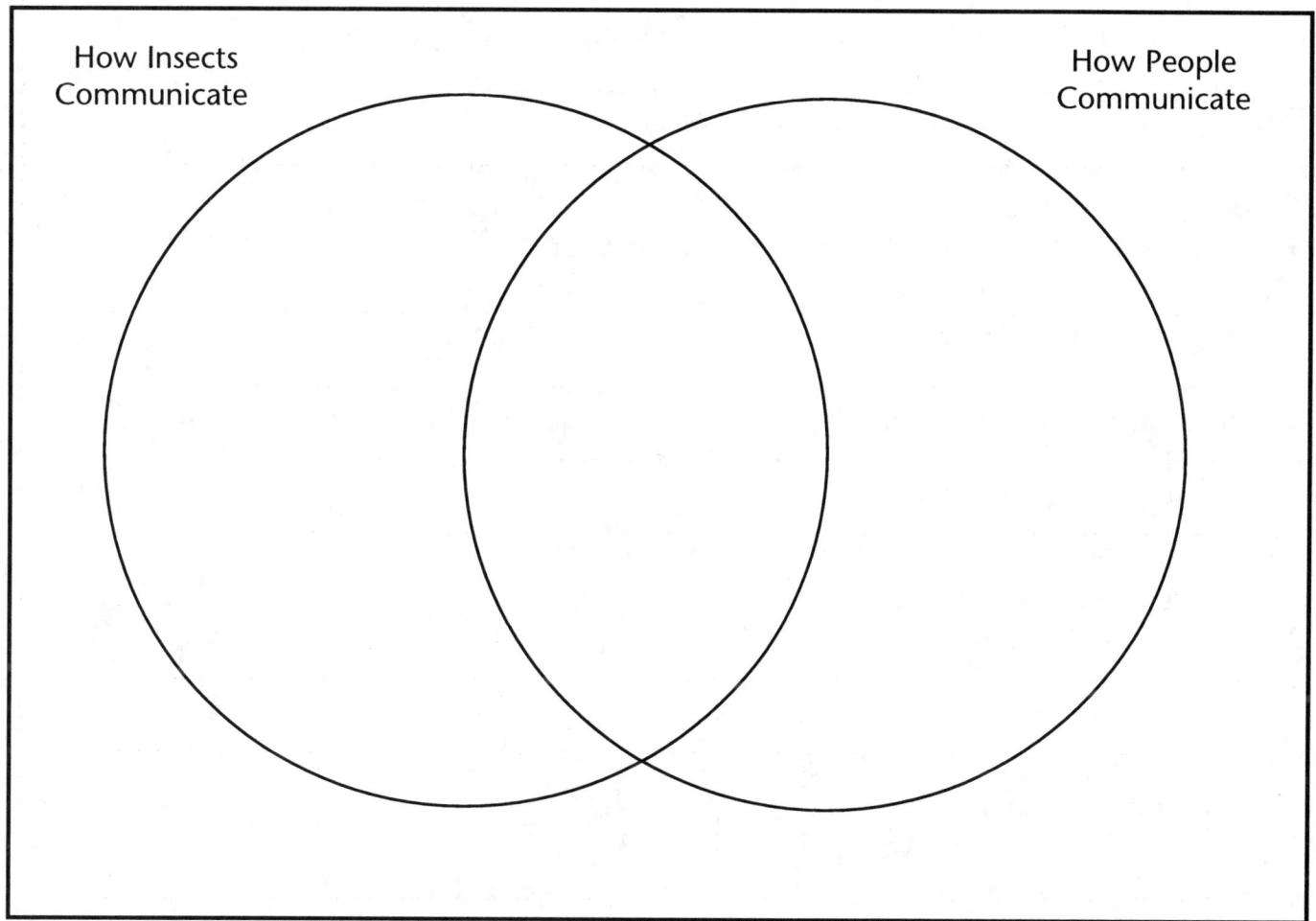

How Insects
Communicate

How People
Communicate

17: The Spider and the Fly

"Won't you come into my parlor?" said the Spider to the Fly,
"It's the **prettiest** little parlor that ever you did spy;
The way into my parlor is up a winding stair,
And I have many curious things to show when you are there."
"Oh no, no," said the little Fly, "to ask me is in vain,
For who goes up your winding stair can never come down again."

"I'm sure you must be **weary**, dear, with soaring up so high;
Will you rest upon my little bed?" said the Spider to the Fly.
"There are pretty curtains drawn around, the **sheets** are fine and thin;
And if you like to rest awhile, I'll snugly tuck you in!"
"Oh no, no," said the little Fly, "for I've often heard it said,
They never, never wake up again, who sleep upon your bed!"

Said the **cunning** Spider to the Fly, "Dear friend, what can I do,
To prove the warm affection I've always felt for you?
I have within my **pantry** good store of all that's nice;
I'm sure you're very welcome—will you please to take a slice?"
"Oh no, no," said the little Fly, "kind sir, that cannot be,
I've heard what's in your pantry, and I do not wish to see."

"Sweet creature," said the Spider, "you're witty and you're wise;
How handsome are your lacy wings, how brilliant are your eyes!"
I have a little looking glass upon my parlor shelf,
If you'll step in a moment, dear, you shall behold yourself."
"I thank you, gentle sir," she said, "for what you're pleased to say,
And bidding you good morning now, I'll call another day."

The Spider turned him round about, and went into his den,
For well he knew the silly Fly would soon come back again;
So he wove a little web, in a little corner sly,
And set his table ready, to dine upon the Fly.
Then he came out to his door again, and merrily did sing;
"Come here, come here, pretty Fly, with the pearl and silver wing;
Your robes are green and purple—there's a crest upon your head;
Your eyes are like the diamonds bright, but mine as dull as lead."

Alas, alas! how very soon this silly little Fly,
Hearing his tricky, flattering words, came slowly flitting by;
With buzzing wings she hung aloft, then near and nearer drew,
Thinking only of her brilliant eyes, and green and purple **hue**;
Thinking only of her crested head—poor foolish thing! At last,
Up jumped the cunning Spider, and fiercely held her fast.
He dragged her up his winding stair, into his dismal den,
Within his little parlor—but she never came out again!

Synonyms/Antonyms (I.D)

1. Which word means about the same as **weary**?

   A Angry
   B Smart
   C High
   D Tired

Context Clues (I.B)

2. In this passage, the word **cunning** means—

   A pretty
   B tricky
   C ugly
   D kind

Synonyms/Antonyms (I.D)

3. Which word means about the same as **pantry**?

   A Ladder
   B Bed
   C Curtains
   D Cupboard

Synonyms/Antonyms (I.D)

4. Which word means about the same as **hue**?

   A Line
   B Size
   C Shape
   D Color

Structural Cues (I.A)

5. What is the root of the word **prettiest**?

   A Pretty
   B Prettier
   C Petting
   D Pretend

Multiple Meanings (I.C)

6. In this passage, the word **sheets** means—

   A pieces of paper
   B bed coverings
   C layers
   D pieces of metal

Facts/Details (II.A)

7. What does the Spider say he has on his parlor shelf?

A Curious things
B Pretty curtains
C Slices of food
D A little looking glass

Sequential Order (II.B)

8. Which of the following happens last in the passage?

A The Spider tells the Fly that there are curious things in his parlor.
B The Fly tells the Spider that those who sleep in the Spider's bed never wake up.
C The Spider jumps on the Fly and drags her up the winding stair.
D The Spider tells the Fly that she has lacy wings and brilliant eyes.

Main Idea (III.A)

9. This passage is mostly about—

A how the Fly escapes from the Spider
B how the Spider tricks the Fly and catches her in his web
C why spiders like to catch flies
D why spiders and flies do not like each other

Cause/Effect (IV.A)

10. The Spider finally catches the Fly because the Fly wants to—

A rest in the Spider's bed
B see inside the Spider's parlor
C see herself in the Spider's looking glass
D eat some of the Spider's food

Generalizations (V.C); Character Analysis (V.D)

11. Which word best describes the Spider?

A Honest
B Unhappy
C Kind
D Clever

Figurative Language (VII.D)

12. In this passage, a spider and fly talk to each other. This is an example of—

A poetry
B rhyme
C comparison
D personification

Figurative Language (VII.D)

13. The Spider says the Fly's eyes are *like diamonds bright*. The phrase *like diamonds bright* is—

A poetry
B personification
C a simile
D a metaphor

Figurative Language (VII.D)

14. The Spider says his own eyes are *as dull as lead*. The phrase *as dull as lead* is—

A a simile

B a metaphor

C personification

D poetry

Similarities/Differences (IV.C)

15. Think about the Spider in this passage. How is the Spider like a real spider? How is the Spider different from a real spider? Use information from the passage in your answer.

Interpretations/Conclusions (V.B)

16. What is the Spider's main problem in this passage? How does he try to solve problem? Is he successful? Why or why not?

Study Skills

VIII. Identify and use sources of different types of information

    A. Use and interpret graphic sources of information

    B. Use reference resources and the parts of a book to locate information

    C. Recognize and use dictionary skills

Practice 1: Study Skills

Directions: Read each question. Then choose the best answer. On your answer sheet, darken the circle for the correct answer.

This is part of the table of contents from a book called *Our World*. Use it to answer the questions.

Contents

Chapter One: The Earth   **5-18**
   What is the earth made of?
   Why are there earthquakes?
   How are rocks formed?
   What are fossils?

Chapter Two: Earth's Weather   **21-28**
   What causes the weather?
   What causes tornadoes and hurricanes?
   World-record weather

Chapter Three: Looking at Seas and Rivers   **32-41**
   Where are the world's oceans?
   What causes tides and waves?
   How are rivers formed?
   How does water affect the earth?

Chapter Four: Earth's Plants   **45-53**
   How do plants make their own food?
   Why do some plants have flowers?
   World-record plants

Chapter Five: Earth's Animals   **56-66**
   What are the main groups of animals?
   How do different animals survive?
   World-record animals

Chapter Six: Earth's Problems   **69-75**
   How do people change the earth?
   How does pollution hurt the earth?
   How can people save the earth?

---

1. Which information would probably be found in Chapter Four?

   A A description of reptiles
   B How plants use sunlight and water
   C How the wind makes waves
   D A description of three kinds of rocks

2. On which page would you begin reading to find out about the weather?

   A 18
   B 21
   C 22
   D 28

3. In which chapter might you read about the world's smallest mammal?

   A Chapter One
   B Chapter Two
   C Chapter Four
   D Chapter Five

4. Which chapter is the longest?

   A Chapter Five
   B Chapter Four
   C Chapter Three
   D Chapter One

5. In which chapter might you read about the kind of rocks in the earth's crust?

   A Chapter Four
   B Chapter Three
   C Chapter Two
   D Chapter One

6. On which page would you begin reading to find out about different kinds of animals?

   A 53
   B 56
   C 66
   D 69

7. Which information would probably be found in Chapter Six?

   A Why people live in cities
   B Why people like animals
   C How people save themselves from storms
   D How people create problems for the earth

8. In which chapter might you read about the world's largest hail stone?

   A Chapter One
   B Chapter Two
   C Chapter Four
   D Chapter Five

Practice 2: Study Skills

Directions: Read each question. Then choose the best answer. On your answer sheet, darken the circle for the correct answer.

This is part of the table of contents from a book of poems. Use it to answer the questions.

Contents

100

1. Which of these poems was written by Eleanor Farjeon?

   A "The Postman"
   B "Snail"
   C "Travel"
   D "Girls' Names"

2. Who wrote the poem "The Little Turtle"?

   A Eleanor Farjeon
   B Laura E. Richards
   C Vachel Lindsay
   D Edna St. Vincent Millay

3. Which two writers wrote poems with the same name?

   A Christopher Marley and Laura E. Richards
   B A.A. Milne and Walter de la Mare
   C Robert Louis Stevenson and Edna St. Vincent Millay
   D Elizabeth Coatsworth and Vachel Lindsay

4. Which poet has the greatest number of poems in this book?

   A Eleanor Farjeon
   B Robert Louis Stevenson
   C Henry Wadsworth Longfellow
   D J.R.R. Tolkien

5. On which page could you find a poem about a bird?

   A page 13
   B page 14
   C page 16
   D page 21

6. Who wrote the poem "Paul Revere's Ride"?

   A Robert Louis Stevenson
   B James Barton Adams
   C Alfred, Lord Tennyson
   D Henry Wadsworth Longfellow

7. Which of these poems was written by Rachel Field?

   A "The Little Turtle"
   B "Whistles"
   C "Boys' Names"
   D "The New Neighbor"

8. A.A. Milne wrote the poem called—

   A "Roads Go Ever Ever On"
   B "Travel"
   C "From a Railway Carriage"
   D "Puppy and I"

Practice 3: Study Skills

Directions: Read each question. Then choose the best answer. On your answer sheet, darken the circle for the correct answer.

This is part of an index from a language arts book. Use it to answer the questions.

Letters,
Addressing the envelope, 166
Business letters, 162-167
Friendly letters, 136-141
Letter to the editor, 147, 151, 162
Punctuation of, 164, 366, 367

Library, 227-235
Card catalog, 228-229
Computer catalog, 231
Reference books, 222-234

Paragraph, 69-81
Kinds of, 72-75
Model paragraphs, 72-75
Moving from one paragraph to
    another, 79
Organizing ideas, 76, 78
Parts of, 70-71
Topic sentence, 70
Using details, 77

1. Toby wants to know how to use the card catalog in the library. On which pages should he look?

   A pp. 227-235
   B pp. 227-230
   C pp. 228-229
   D pp. 231

2. To find the kind of letter he might write to his friend in New York, Toby should look on—

   A pp. 227-235
   B pp. 162-167
   C pp. 136-141
   D pp. 72-75

3. Toby wants to know about writing paragraphs that describe. He should be reading page—

   A 69
   B 70
   C 71
   D 72

4. During the next two weeks, Toby's class will learn about writing paragraphs. Which pages in their language arts book will they probably read?

   A pp. 69-81
   B pp. 70-71
   C pp. 162-167
   D pp. 227-235

Practice 4: Study Skills

Directions: Read each question. Then choose the best answer. On your answer sheet, darken the circle for the correct answer.

This is part of an index from a math book. Use it to answer the questions.

Addition
　with regrouping, 156-163
　estimating answers, 28-29
　of money, 166-170

Circle, 318-319
　center of, 318
　using a compass, 318-319

Drawing
　circles, 318, 319
　rectangles, 314-315
　squares, 314-315

Estimating answers
　addition, 28-29
　subtraction, 38-40

Fractions, 240-245
　comparing, 244-245
　using pictures to show, 240-243

Graphs, 196-215
　bar, 202-206
　circle, 207-211
　line, 212-215
　picture, 196-201

1. On which pages could you learn about bar graphs?

　A pp. 196-201
　B pp. 196-215
　C pp. 202-206
　D pp. 240-243

2. On which pages could you learn about using a compass?

　A pp. 318-319
　B pp. 244-245
　C pp. 212-215
　D pp. 156-163

3. How many different kinds of graphs does this book include?

　A 0
　B 2
　C 3
　D 4

4. To learn how to estimate answers in subtraction, you would look on pages—

　A 28-29
　B 28-40
　C 28-38
　D 38-40

Practice 5: Study Skills

Directions: Read each question. Then choose the best answer. On your answer sheet, darken the circle for the correct answer.

1. To find out how to pronounce a word, you should look in—

   A an atlas
   B a newspaper
   C a dictionary
   D an encyclopedia

2. To find when a movie is showing at a local theater, you should look in—

   A an atlas
   B a newspaper
   C an encyclopedia
   D a telephone book

3. To find several words that are synonyms for *hot*, you could look in—

   A a thesaurus
   B as atlas
   C a newspaper
   D an encyclopedia

4. To find information for a report about how mountains are formed, you could look—

   A in the newspaper
   B in an encyclopedia
   C in a dictionary
   D on a globe

5. To find out whether a word is a noun or a verb, you should look in—

   A an encyclopedia
   B a telephone book
   C a dictionary
   D a newspaper

6. To find out when a special about tigers will show on television, you should look in—

   A a dictionary
   B a magazine
   C an atlas
   D a newspaper

7. To find the distance from your home town to the state capitol, you would probably use a—

   A globe
   B city map
   C state map
   D world map

8. You want to know the population of New York City for the past ten years. To find this information, you should look in—

   A a magazine
   B an atlas
   C an encyclopedia
   D an almanac

Practice 6: Study Skills

Directions: Read each question. Then choose the best answer. On your answer sheet, darken the circle for the correct answer.

This is the title page from a book about taking tests. Use it to answer the questions.

Learning How
to Take Tests

Doing Better Than
You Ever Thought You Could!

by Jeffrey T. Martin

Illustrations by Melanie Johnson

Lori Moore, Editor

© 1998

Better Learning Books
Columbus, Ohio

Printed in the U.S.A.

1. This book is probably about—

   A choosing a good school
   B improving test-taking skills
   C pleasing your parents and
      teachers
   D writing test questions for fun

2. Who wrote this book?

   A Better Learning Books
   B Lori Moore
   C Melanie Johnson
   D Jeffrey T. Martin

3. 1998 is the year that this book
   was—

   A written
   B placed in the library
   C bought
   D published

4. The title page explains—

   A how long it should take to read
      the book
   B where the book was printed
   C why the authors wrote the book
   D how to take tests

5. The subtitle for this book is—

   A Better Learning Books
   B Learning How to Take Tests
   C Doing Better Than You Ever
      Thought You Could!
   D Learning How to Do Better

6. Who drew the pictures included
   in this book?

   A Jeffrey T. Martin
   B Lori Moore
   C Melanie Johnson
   D Better Learning Books

Practice 7: Study Skills

Directions: Read each question. Then choose the best answer. On your answer sheet, darken the circle for the correct answer.

At the library, Debra used the computer card catalog to find some books about basketball. Here are the title cards for two of the books Debra found. Use them to answer the questions.

Card 1

Juvenile Fiction

Title	The million dollar shot/Dan Gutman
Author	Gutman, Dan
Publisher	New York: Hyperion Books for Children, c 1997.
Description	114 pp.
Summary	Eleven-year-old Eddie gets a chance to win a million dollars by sinking a foul shot at the National Basketball Association (NBA) finals.
Subject(s)	Basketball fiction
	Contests fiction
	Wealth fiction
Format	Juvenile

Card 2

796.323

Title	The story of basketball/Dave Anderson; foreward by Grant Hill
Author	Anderson, Dave
Publisher	New York: W. Morrow, c 1997
Description	144 pp., illustrated
Notes	Includes index
Summary	Presents an overview of the history of basketball from its beginning in 1891 and profiles some famous players and coaches of modern times.
Subject(s)	Basketball history
	Basketball players
Format	Juvenile

107

1. Who wrote *The Million Dollar Shot?*

   A Grant Hill
   B Dave Anderson
   C Dan Gutman
   D W. Morrow

2. *The Story of Basketball* was published in—

   A 1891
   B 1944
   C 1995
   D 1997

3. *The Story of Basketball* is about—

   A learning to play basketball
   B the rules of basketball
   C a boy who tries to win a basketball contest
   D where and when basketball began

4. Which of these is NOT true?

   A *The Million Dollar Shot* is fiction.
   B *The Story of Basketball* has 144 pages.
   C *The Story of Basketball* does not have pictures in it.
   D *The Million Dollar Shot* was published by Hyperion Books

5. To find other books like *The Story of Basketball,* Debra could look under the following category of books:

   A Basketball fiction
   B Contests fiction
   C Basketball history
   D Juvenile

6. *The Million Dollar Shot* is about—

   A how Dan Gutman became a basketball star
   B why basketball players earn so much money
   C how the game of basketball began
   D how a boy has a chance to win a million dollars at a basketball game

Practice 8: Study Skills

Directions: Read each question. Then choose the best answer. On your answer sheet, darken the circle for the correct answer.

At the library, Mike used the computer card catalog to find some books about guide dogs. Here are the title cards for two of the books Mike found. Use them to answer the questions.

Card 1

362.41	
Title	Mom's best friend/Sally Hobart Alexander; photographs by George Ancona
Author	Alexander, Sally Hobart
Publisher	New York: MacMillan, c 1992
Description	45 pp., illustrated
Subject(s)	Guide dogs
Other	
Entries	Ancona, George, illustrator
Format	Juvenile

Card 2

362.4	
Title	A guide dog goes to school: the story of a dog trained to lead the blind/ Elizabeth Simpson Smith; illustrated by Bert Dodson
Author	Smith, Elizabeth Simpson
Publisher	New York: W. Morrow, c 1987
Description	51 pp., illustrated
Notes	Includes index
Subject(s)	Guide dogs
Other	
Entries	Dodson, Bert, illustrator
Format	Juvenile

1. Who wrote *Mom's Best Friend?*

   A George Ancona
   B Elizabeth Simpson Smith
   C Bert Dodson
   D Sally Hobart Alexander

2. Which of these is NOT true?

   A Both books were published by the same company.
   B Both books have pictures.
   C *Mom's Best Friend* was published in 1992.
   D *A Guide Dog Goes to School* has an index.

3. Both of these books—

   A have the same number of pages
   B were written by the same person
   C are about the same subject
   D were published in the same year

4. *A Guide Dog Goes to School* was published in—

   A 1945
   B 1951
   C 1987
   D 1992

5. Who took the pictures used in *Mom's Best Friend?*

   A Sally Hobart Alexander
   B Bert Dodson
   C George Ancona
   D Elizabeth Simpson Smith

6. What is the copyright year for *Mom's Best Friend?*

   A 1992
   B 1987
   C 1951
   D 1945

Practice 9: Study Skills

Directions: Read each question. Then choose the best answer. On your answer sheet, darken the circle for the correct answer.

The graph shows the amount of rain that fell during a five-year period. Use the graph to answer the questions.

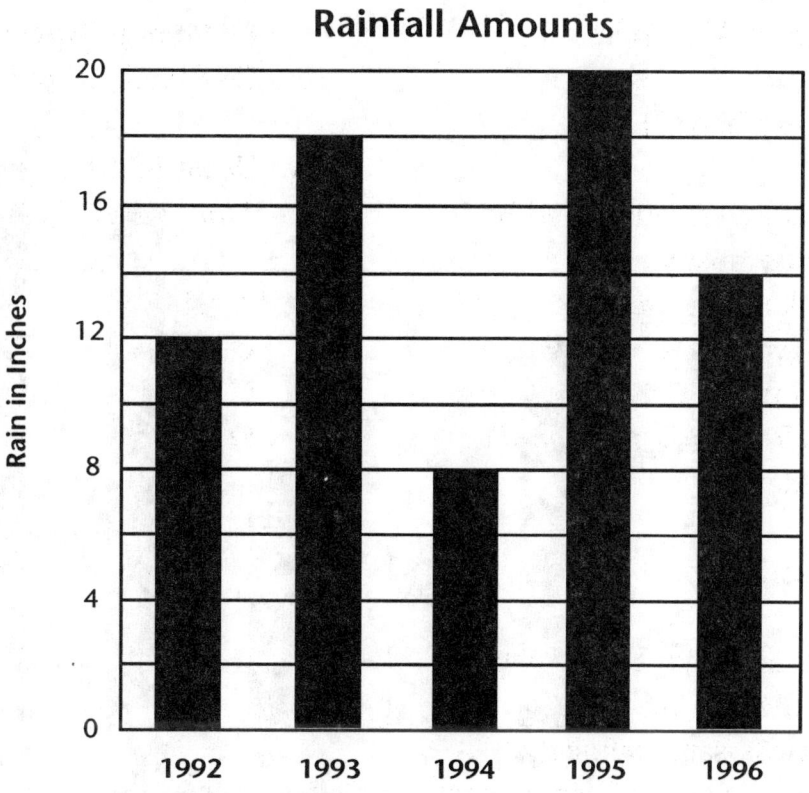

Rainfall Amounts

1. In which year did the greatest amount of rain fall?

   A 1996
   B 1995
   C 1994
   D 1993

2. What was the total amount of rain that fell during 1993 and 1994?

   A 26 inches
   B 18 inches
   C 12 inches
   D 10 inches

3. How many inches of rain fell in 1996?

   A 14 inches
   B 12 inches
   C 10 inches
   D 8 inches

4. How much more rain fell during 1992 than in 1994?

   A 20 inches
   B 12 inches
   C 8 inches
   D 4 inches

©ECS Learning Systems, Inc.

111

Practice 10: Study Skills

Directions: Read each question. Then choose the best answer. On your answer sheet, darken the circle for the correct answer.

The graph shows the number of hours several children spent watching television during May. Use the graph to answer the questions.

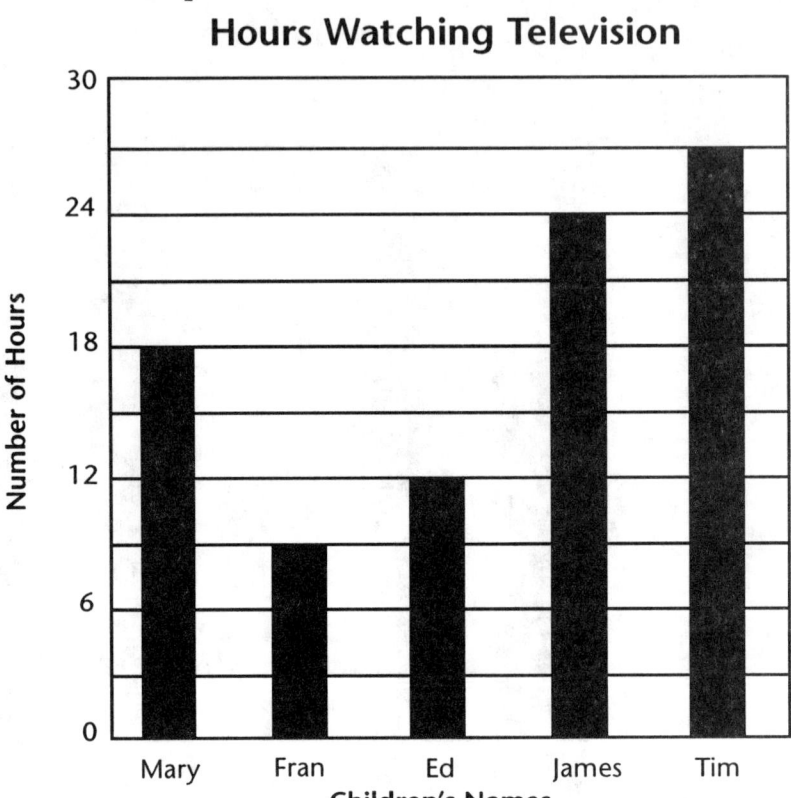

Hours Watching Television

1. How many hours of television did Mary watch during May?

   A 6
   B 12
   C 15
   D 18

2. Which child watched the least television during May?

   A Ed
   B Fran
   C James
   D Tim

3. What was the total number of hours Ed and James spent watching television?

   A 12
   B 24
   C 30
   D 36

4. How many more hours of televsion did Tim watch than Fran?

   A 27
   B 18
   C 12
   D 9

Practice 11: Study Skills

Directions: Read each question. Then choose the best answer. On your answer sheet, darken the circle for the correct answer.

Here is the dictionary entry for the word **limit**. Use it to answer the questions.

limit [lim´it] *noun, plural* **limits. 1.** the place where something stops or ends: *She walked to the outer* **limit** *of the yard.* **2. limits.** The edge of an area: *Where are the city's* **limits. 3.** the most that is allowed: *The boy ate his* **limit** *of candy.* *–verb,* **limited, limiting.** to place a limit: ***Limit*** *your time on the telephone.*

1. The word **limit** can be either a noun or—

   A an adjective
   B an adverb
   C a verb
   D a pronoun

2. What does the word **limit** mean in the following sentence?

   *You should **limit** the amount of sodas you drink.*

   A the place where something stops
   B the outer part of something
   C the edge of an area
   D to place a limit

3. What is the plural of the word **limit**?

   A limited
   B limiting
   C limits
   D [lim´it]

4. Which of these could be the guide words in a dictionary for the word limit ?

   A lace-land
   B lead-leash
   C lime-limp
   D lucky-lumber

5. What does the word **limit** mean in the following sentence?

   *Josh passed the **limit** of five absences in one month.*

   A the place where something stops
   B the most that is allowed
   C the edge of an area
   D to place a limit

Practice 12: Study Skills

Directions: Read each question. Then choose the best answer. On your answer sheet, darken the circle for the correct answer.

Here is a dictionary entry for the word **curtain**. Use it to answer the questions.

curtain [kur´tn] *noun, plural* **curtains**. **1.** a large cloth hung across a room. **2.** a large hanging cloth that separates a stage from the audience. **3.** anything that covers or hides something else like a curtain: *A **curtain** of smoke hung in the air.* *–verb*, **curtained**, **curtaining**. to hang a curtain: *My mother **curtained** off part of the basement.*

1. What is the meaning of **curtain** in the following sentence?

   *The actor looked at us from behind the **curtain**.*

   A a large cloth hung across a room
   B to hang a curtain
   C something that covers or hides something
   D a large hanging cloth that separates a stage from an audience

2. Which of these could be the guide words for the word **curtain** in a dictionary?

   A credit-creep
   B cross-crown
   C curry-cushion
   D cycle-czar

3. The plural of the word **curtain** is—

   A curtain
   B curtains
   C curtained
   D curtaining

4. The word **curtain** can be a verb or—

   A an adverb
   B an adjective
   C a noun
   D a pronoun

5. What is the meaning of **curtain** in the following sentence?

   *I want to **curtain** off that part of my bedroom.*

   A a large cloth hung across a room
   B to hang a curtain
   C something that covers or hides something
   D a large hanging cloth that separates a stage from an audience

Practice 13: Study Skills

Directions: Look at the map. Then read each question and choose the best answer. On your answer sheet, darken the circle for the correct answer.

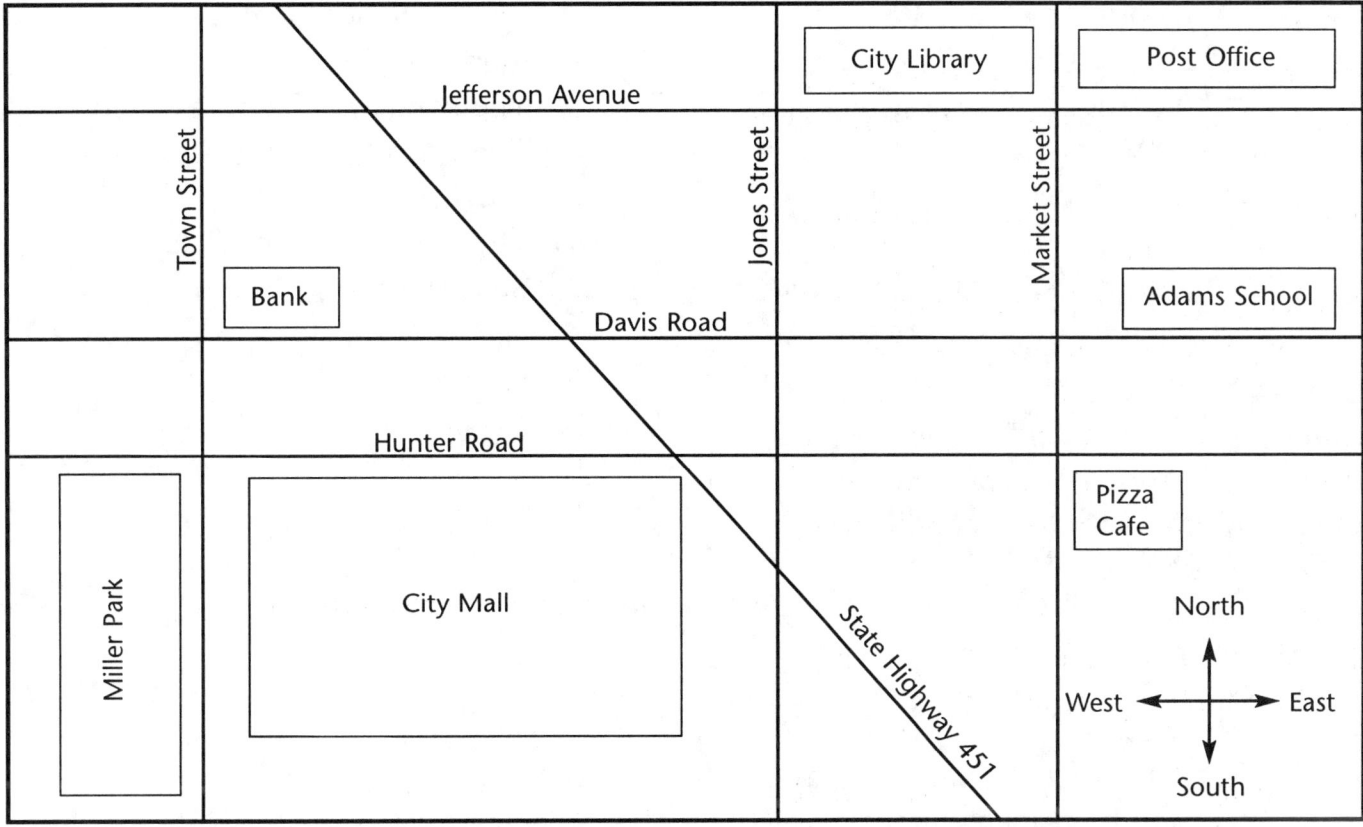

1. Annie wants to walk to the bank from Adams School. She should walk—

   A south on Market Street
   B north on Market Street
   C west on Davis Road
   D east on Davis Road

2. The city library is located on—

   A Davis Road
   B Town Street
   C State Highway 451
   D Jefferson Avenue

3. Mark must take a package to the post office. He begins walking from Miller Park at the corner of Town Street and Hunter Road. Which of the following routes will take him to the post office?

   A East on Hunter Road and then south on Jones Street
   B North on Town Street and then west on Jefferson Avenue
   C East on Hunter Road and then North on Market Street
   D East on Hunter Road and then northwest on State Highway 451

©ECS Learning Systems, Inc.

115

4. The Pizza Cafe is located—

A on State Highway 451
B at the corner of Market Street and Hunter Road
C at the corner of Hunter Road and Jones Street
D on Town Street

5. After going to the library, Jody and her friends plan to go for pizza. Which of the following routes will take them to the Pizza Cafe?

A South on Jones Street and then west on Davis Road
B South on Market Street to Hunter Road
C South on Market Street and then west on Hunter Road
D West on Jefferson Avenue and then south on Jones Street

6. Which two places are both located on Jefferson Avenue?

A Adams School and the city library
B The bank and the post office
C The city library and the post office
D The post office and Adams School

Appendix

- **Answer Key**
- **Scoring Guidelines for Open-Ended Questions**
- **Scoring Rubrics for Open-Ended Questions**
- **Vocabulary List**
- **Answer Sheet**

Answer Key: Vocabulary

Practice 1 (p. 12)
1. D **2.** B **3.** C **4.** B **5.** A
6. D **7.** C **8.** B **9.** B **10.** D

Practice 2 (p. 13)
1. C **2.** A **3.** C **4.** C **5.** A
6. B **7.** C **8.** A **9.** B **10.** B

Practice 3 (p. 14)
1. D **2.** C **3.** C **4.** D **5.** A
6. C **7.** D **8.** C **9.** B **10.** D

Practice 4 (p. 15)
1. C **2.** D **3.** A **4.** C **5.** B
6. B **7.** D **8.** B **9.** D **10.** A

Practice 5 (p. 16)
1. B **2.** C **3.** B **4.** D **5.** C
6. B **7.** B **8.** A **9.** D **10.** D

Practice 6 (p. 17)
1. B **2.** C **3.** C **4.** B **5.** D
6. A **7.** C **8.** C **9.** B **10.** D

Practice 7 (p. 18)
1. C **2.** B **3.** D **4.** C **5.** B
6. A **7.** D **8.** B

Practice 8 (p. 19)
1. B **2.** C **3.** C **4.** A **5.** D
6. C **7.** B **8.** B

Practice 9 (p. 20)
1. D **2.** A **3.** C **4.** C **5.** B
6. B **7.** D **8.** B

Practice 10 (p. 21)
1. C **2.** C **3.** B **4.** D **5.** A
6. D **7.** B **8.** D

Practice 11 (p. 22)
1. D **2.** A **3.** B **4.** C **5.** C
6. D

Practice 12 (p. 23)
1. D **2.** C **3.** B **4.** C **5.** A
6. B

Answer Key: Comprehension

1: The Safe Way to Fly a Kite (p. 26)
1. C **2.** B **3.** B **4.** C **5.** B
6. A **7.** C **8.** D **9.** B **10.** C
11. B **12.** A **13.** D **14.** See scoring guidelines and rubrics

2: What Do the Months Bring? (p. 30)
1. B **2.** C **3.** C **4.** D **5.** A
6. C **7.** C **8.** A **9.** D **10.** C
11. See scoring guidelines and rubrics

3: Food Named After People (p. 33)
1. D **2.** D **3.** C **4.** C **5.** A
6. D **7.** B **8.** C **9.** A **10.** C
11. D **12. & 13.** See scoring guidelines and rubrics

4: Larks in the Cornfield (p. 37)
1. C **2.** A **3.** C **4.** B **5.** C
6. B **7.** C **8.** B **9.** D **10.** D
11. C **12.** D **13.** See scoring guidelines and rubrics

5: Birbal and the Six Foolish People Part 1 (p. 41)
1. D **2.** B **3.** A **4.** C **5.** B
6. A **7.** D **8.** C **9.** B **10.** D
11. C **12.** D **13.** C **14. & 15.** See scoring guidelines and rubrics

6: Birbal and the Six Foolish People Part 2 (p. 46)
1. C **2.** C **3.** B **4.** D **5.** C
6. D **7.** B **8.** A **9.** C
10. & 11. See scoring guidelines and rubrics

7: What Kind of Pet Is It? (p. 50)
1. B 2. C 3. B 4. B 5. C
6. D 7. D 8. A 9. C 10. B
11. C 12. & 13. See scoring guidelines and rubrics

8: Be Water-Wise (p. 54)
1. A 2. D 3. B 4. D 5. B
6. D 7. B 8. A 9. C 10. B
11. D 12. See scoring guidelines and rubrics

9: Beautiful Bluebonnets (p. 58)
1. C 2. D 3. C 4. D 5. D
6. C 7. C 8. B 9. A 10. C
11. & 12. See scoring guidelines and rubrics

10: My Early Home (p. 63)
1. B 2. D 3. D 4. C 5. C
6. A 7. C 8. B 9. D 10. B
11. C 12. D 13. & 14. See scoring guidelines and rubrics

11: Around and Around (p. 68)
1. B 2. C 3. D 4. A 5. C
6. A 7. D 8. C 9. See scoring guidelines and rubrics

12: Rainbow Happiness (p. 71)
1. B 2. C 3. D 4. A 5. D
6. C 7. B 8. A 9. C 10. D
11. C 12. & 13. See scoring guidelines and rubrics

13: How to Wrap a Present (p. 76)
1. D 2. C 3. B 4. D 5. C
6. B 7. A 8. C 9. B 10. C
11. See scoring guidelines and rubrics

14: A Different Kind of Bird (p. 80)
1. A 2. C 3. B 4. B 5. D
6. C 7. B 8. C 9. B 10. D
11. C 12. C 13. See scoring guidelines and rubrics

15: The Elves and the Shoemaker (p. 84)
1. D 2. A 3. B 4. A 5. C
6. C 7. D 8. A 9. C 10. B
11. C 12. See scoring guidelines and rubrics

16: Insect Languages (p. 88)
1. B 2. C 3. A 4. D 5. C
6. C 7. D 8. D 9. & 10. See scoring guidelines and rubrics

17: The Spider and the Fly (p. 92)
1. D 2. B 3. D 4. D 5. A
6. B 7. D 8. C 9. B 10. C
11. D 12. D 13. C 14. A
15. & 16. See scoring guidelines and rubrics

Answer Key: Study Skills

Practice 1 (p. 98)
1. B 2. B 3. D 4. D 5. D
6. B 7. D 8. B

Practice 2 (p. 100)
1. D 2. C 3. C 4. B 5. C
6. D 7. B 8. D

Practice 3 (p. 102)
1. C 2. C 3. D 4. A

Practice 4 (p. 103)
1. C 2. A 3. D 4. D

Practice 5 (p. 104)
1. C 2. B 3. A 4. B 5. C
6. D 7. C 8. D

Practice 6 (p. 105)
1. B 2. D 3. D 4. B 5. C
6. C

Practice 7 (p. 107)
1. C 2. D 3. D 4. C 5. C
6. D

Practice 8 (p. 109)

1. D   **2.** A   **3.** C   **4.** C   **5.** C

6. A

Practice 9 (p. 111)

1. B   **2.** A   **3.** A   **4.** D

Practice 10 (p. 112)

1. D   **2.** B   **3.** D   **4.** B

Practice 11 (p. 113)

1. C   **2.** D   **3.** C   **4.** C   **5.** B

Practice 12 (p. 114)

1. D   **2.** C   **3.** B   **4.** C   **5.** B

Practice 13 (p. 115)

1. C   **2.** D   **3.** C   **4.** B   **5.** B

6. C

Scoring Guidelines for Open-Ended Questions

Author's Purpose

An effective response will include the following elements—

- an introduction that clearly states the writer's position
- a clear, effective organizational plan
- evidence of writer's careful study of text's message
- appropriate and specific reasons that logically support the writer's position
- clear, logical elaboration of reasons with facts, details, examples, information, etc., from the text
- a clear, logical conclusion that summarizes the writer's position and supporting evidence

Use these scoring guidelines with the following open-ended question—

"Food Named After People," page 36, #13

Character Analysis

An effective response will include the following elements—

- an introduction that presents the writer's overall impression of the character
- a clear, consistent focus on one character
- specific details (e.g., the character's words, the character's actions) that identify/describe the character
- a clear, logical conclusion that brings closure to the response

Use these scoring guidelines with the following open-ended questions—

"My Early Home," page 67, #14
"Rainbow Happiness," page 74, #12

Genre Identification

When identifying the correct genre of a reading selection, students should mention several of the following characteristics—

Fiction
- use of the basic elements (character, setting, problem, solution)
- sequence of events leading to a resolution (plot)
- purpose: to entertain

Nonfiction
- emphasis on factual events/information
- purpose: to explain, argue, persuade

Poetry
- use of stanza/verse form
- focus on sounds of language (e.g., alliteration, onomatopoeia)
- use of figurative language (e.g., similes, metaphors)
- use of rhyme and rhythm

Use these scoring guidelines with the following open-ended questions—

"The Safe Way to Fly a Kite," page 29, #14
"What Do the Months Bring?" page 32, #11
"Food Named After People," page 35, #12
"What Kind of Pet Is It?" page 52, #12

Interpretations/Conclusions

An effective response will include the following elements—

- an introduction that clearly states the writer's opinion
- a clear, effective organizational plan
- appropriate and specific reasons that logically support the writer's position
- clear and logical elaboration of reasons with facts, details, information, etc., from the text
- clear transitions from one part of the answer to another
- a clear, logical conclusion that summarizes the writer's position and reasons

Use these scoring guidelines with the following open-ended questions—

"Larks in the Cornfield," page 40, #13
"What Kind of Pet Is It?" page 53, #13
"Beautiful Bluebonnets," page 61, #11
"Rainbow Happiness," page 75, #13
"A Different Kind of Bird," page 83, #13
"The Spider and the Fly," page 96, #16

Main Idea

An effective response will include the following elements—

- an introduction that presents the new title created by the writer
- a clear, effective organizational plan
- appropriate and specific reasons that logically support the suggested title
- clear transitions from one part of the answer to another
- a clear, logical conclusion that summarizes the writer's reasons for the suggested title

Use these scoring guidelines with the following open-ended questions—

"Birbal and the Six Foolish People, Part 2"
    page 48, #10
"My Early Home," page 66, #13

Predictions

An effective response will include the following elements—

- an introduction that clearly states the predicted outcome
- a clear, effective organizational plan
- appropriate and specific reasons that logically support the writer's prediction
- clear, logical elaboration of reasons with facts, details, information, etc., from the text
- a clear, logical conclusion that summarizes the writer's prediction and supporting reasons

Use these scoring guidelines with the following open-ended questions—

"Birbal and the Six Foolish People, Part 1,"
    page 44, #14
"Be Water-Wise," page 57, #12

Sequential Order

An effective response will include the following elements—

- an introduction that clearly states the composition's topic/focus
- a clear, effective organizational plan
- specific, delineated steps (in a process) or events (of a narrative)
- consistent use of chronological order
- clear statements of cause-effect relationships
- clear transitions from one step/event to another
- specific details that clarify each step/event
- a clear, logical conclusion that brings closure to the writing

Use these scoring guidelines with the following open-ended questions—

"Birbal and the Six Foolish People, Part 1," page 45, #15
"Around and Around," page 70, #9
"How to Wrap a Present," page 79, #11

Similarities/Differences

An effective response will include the following elements—

- an introduction that clearly identifies the issues, characters, items, etc., to be compared and/or contrasted
- a clear, effective organizational plan to handle both similarities and/or differences
- specific details that identify similarities and/or differences
- clear transitions from one part of the response to another
- a clear, logical conclusion that summarizes the points made in the response

Use these scoring guidelines with the following open-ended questions—

"Birbal and the Six Foolish People, Part 2," page 49, #11*
"Beautiful Bluebonnets," page 62, #12
"The Elves and the Shoemaker," page 87, #12*
"Insect Languages," page 91, #10*
"The Spider and the Fly," page 95, #15

*These questions do not require a written composition as a response. To evaluate them, focus on the student's selection and use of specific details that identify similarities and differences.

Summarize Ideas

An effective response will include the following elements—

- a clear focus on the text's major ideas
- omission of extraneous details/information
- a clear, accurate statement of the text's basic message/content

Use these scoring guidelines with the following open-ended question—

"Insect Languages," page 90, #9

Scoring Rubrics for Open-Ended Questions

In most states that administer tests with open-ended questions requiring student-written responses, evaluators use scoring rubrics to assess these responses. A scoring rubric is an assessment tool designed to determine the degree to which a writer meets the established criteria for a given writing task.

Many scoring rubrics allow for holistic evaluation, which focuses on the overall effectiveness of the written response rather than individual errors in content, organization, mechanics, etc. For example, a scoring rubric might allow a teacher to score papers on a scale from 1 (for the least effective responses) to 4 (for the most effective responses). Rubrics that offer a broader scale of points (e.g., 1–6) allow for a more refined evaluation of a written response. For example, with these rubrics it is possible for evaluators to distinguish between an outstanding response (e.g., 6) and a very good response (e.g., 5). Rubrics with a narrow scale of points (e.g., 0–2) do not allow for a very refined evaluation, generally limiting evaluators to a response of either "pass" or "fail."

Sample scoring rubrics appear on the following pages. They offer several options for evaluating the written responses students complete for the open-ended questions in *TestSMART*™. A brief description of each rubric follows.

Note: Teachers may also use scoring rubrics provided for their own state's competency test.

Three-point rubric: This rubric has a narrow scale of points and, therefore, limits the scoring to basically pass–fail. The two-point rubric is most appropriate for brief written responses (2-4 sentences). In addition, this rubric works well with the short answers recorded on graphic organizers (e.g., Venn diagrams).

Four-point rubric: This rubric provides a wider scale of points, making a more refined evaluation possible. It does not, however, allow teachers to make clear distinctions between outstanding responses and those that are merely good. The four-point rubric is appropriate for brief written responses (2-4 sentences) and longer responses (two or more paragraphs).

Six-point rubric: Because of the broad scale of points, this rubric allows for a more refined evaluation of a written response. The six-point rubric is appropriate for longer responses (two or more paragraphs).

Three-Point Rubric

2 Provides complete, appropriate response
Shows a thorough understanding
Exhibits logical reasoning/conclusions
Presents an accurate and complete response

1 Provides a partly inappropriate response
Includes flawed reasoning/incorrect conclusions
Overlooks part of question/task
Presents an incomplete response
Shows incomplete understanding

0 Indicates no understanding of reading selection
Fails to respond to question/task

Four-Point Rubric

4 Focus on topic throughout response
Thorough, complete ideas/information
Clear organization throughout
Logical reasoning/conclusions
Thorough understanding of reading task
Accurate, complete response

3 Focus on topic throughout most of response
Many relevant ideas/pieces of information
Clear organization throughout most of response
Minor problems in logical reasoning/conclusions
General understanding of reading task
Generally accurate and complete response

2 Minimal focus on topic/task
Minimally relevant ideas/information
Obvious gaps in organization
Obvious problems in logical reasoning/conclusions
Minimal understanding of reading task
Inaccuracies/incomplete response

1 Little or no focus on topic/task
Irrelevant ideas/information
No coherent organization
Major problems in logical reasoning/conclusions
Little or no understanding of reading task
Generally inaccurate/incomplete response

Six-Point Rubric

6
Full focus on topic throughout response
Thorough, complete ideas/information
Clear, maintained organizational pattern throughout
Clearly logical reasoning/conclusions
Thorough understanding of reading task
Accurate, complete response

5
Focus on topic throughout most of response
Very thorough ideas/information
Clear organization throughout majority of response
Generally logical reasoning/conclusions
Overall understanding of reading task
Generally accurate and complete response

4
Focus on topic/task but with obvious minor digressions
Sufficient relevant ideas/information
Minor gaps in organization in parts of response
Minor problems in logical reasoning/conclusions
Above average understanding of reading task
Minor inaccuracies that affect quality and thoroughness of response

3
Focus on topic/task but with obvious major digressions
Relevant ideas/information mixed with irrelevant material
Major gaps in organization
Somewhat logical reasoning/conclusions
Basic understanding of reading task
Several inaccuracies that affect quality and thoroughness of response

2
Little or no focus on topic/task throughout response
Few relevant ideas/pieces of information included in response
Lack of organizational plan
Illogical reasoning/conclusions throughout response
Lack of basic understanding of reading task
Generally inaccurate/incomplete response

1
Unacceptable response due to severe problems in focus, relevancy, organization, and/or logical reasoning/conclusions
No understanding of reading task

Vocabulary List

accept	cluster	halt	polish	speck
account	colony	harmony	pray	spur
accuse	comfort	humbly	prayer	stagger
accustom	compass	instant	preserve	statue
adapt	complain	ivory	prey	sturdy
advantage	conduct	keen	probably	style
adventurous	conquer	knit	product	support
advertise	conqueror	laboratory	professor	swear
affection	contrast	lane	program	sword
afford	convince	lash	protect	terrify
alfalfa	cottage	lest	protection	thigh
anchor	couple	limber	quality	tingle
angle	curly	linen	quarrel	tobacco
annual	delightful	loaf	queer	tuft
antler	detective	lynx	quiver	vast
approach	diamond	magnet	reed	velvet
argument	ease	marble	register	venture
arrest	educate	mast	regular	verse
astronaut	education	mayor	relative	vessel
backwoods	electric	medicine	religion	victim
bacon	electricity	melody	represent	waist
banner	exchange	melon	require	whisk
basin	excite	memory	respect	wilderness
blizzard	excuse	modest	responsible	witness
blush	exhaust	monk	ripple	zone
bodyguard	exit	mosquito	rival	
breed	extend	mumble	saddle	
bronze	fame	odor	salute	
brow	fashion	official	satisfy	
bullet	feeble	oxygen	sausage	
bureau	flatter	oyster	scale	
bushel	flush	parcel	scamper	
canal	freight	particular	scorn	
card	freshwater	pastor	shabby	
carpenter	gentleman	patent	shield	
cauliflower	gentlemen	patient	shower	
celebrate	glide	peak	shutter	
challenge	glum	pearl	sift	
champion	goal	percent	signal	
channel	gobble	perfect	similar	
chemistry	godparent	picket	sink	
cleverness	groan	plaster	situation	
climate	grocery	pliers	slither	
cloak	grunt	plum	slope	
clump	hail	poison	spare	

Name _____ **Date** _____

Vocabulary: Practice # _____   **Study Skills:** Practice # _____
Comprehension: Passage # _____

Answer Sheet

1. (A) (B) (C) (D)   8. (A) (B) (C) (D)

2. (A) (B) (C) (D)   9. (A) (B) (C) (D)

3. (A) (B) (C) (D)   10. (A) (B) (C) (D)

4. (A) (B) (C) (D)   11. (A) (B) (C) (D)

5. (A) (B) (C) (D)   12. (A) (B) (C) (D)

6. (A) (B) (C) (D)   13. (A) (B) (C) (D)

7. (A) (B) (C) (D)   14. (A) (B) (C) (D)